AIR FRYER

everyday recipes

Delicious recipes for daily
meals and snacks

pil

Publications International, Ltd.

Some of the products listed in this publication may be in limited distribution.

Pictured on the front cover *(clockwise from top left)*: Apple Pie Egg Rolls *(page 182)*, Crispy Brussels Sprouts *(page 122)*, and Bang-Bang Cauliflower *(page 118)*.

Photograph on top right © Shutterstock.com.

Pictured on the back cover *(clockwise from top left)*: Air-Fried Pepperoni Pizza Bagels *(page 148)*, Crispy Mushrooms *(page 16)*, Fried Pineapple with Toasted Coconut *(page 176)*, and Ricotta Pancakes *(page 34)*.

ISBN: 978-1-63938-137-1

Manufactured in China.

8 7 6 5 4 3 2 1

Microwave Cooking: Microwave ovens vary in wattage. Use the cooking times as guidelines and check for doneness before adding more time.

Let's get social!
@Publications_International
@PublicationsInternational
www.pilbooks.com

CONTENTS

introduction 4

appetizers and starters 6

breakfast 32

light meals 48

dinner 76

sides 108

kids' favorites 140

snacks 160

sweets and treats 174

index 189

INTRODUCTION

Do you enjoy cooking a variety of foods but often can't find the time? Or, do you just need ideas for preparing everyday meals for you and your family?

Your air fryer is here to help. You'll learn to prepare many of the foods you love and crave while realizing that your air fryer is easy to use, cooks food faster and provides a no-fuss clean up.

You may have thought that your air fryer only prepares healthier "fried foods," but you'll soon find that you can prepare all types of other foods in it, too. Prepare everything from appetizers to meals to sides and even desserts! Why not try pizza or sandwiches? Maybe, a tasty chicken breast or marinated salmon to top your favorite salad or as a main dish? Or, how about a side of roasted vegetables? You'll soon realize how versatile your air fryer is—from baking to grilling, steaming, roasting, and reheating.

Choose from more than 100 of your favorite dishes here, or try to create your own. Once you learn how to use your air fryer, you'll realize how easy it is to master it.

Now, enjoy your favorite foods at home. Plus, as an added benefit, you'll have the recipes at your fingertips to prepare over and over again!

helpful tips

- Read your air fryer's manufacturer's directions carefully before cooking to make sure you understand the specific features of your air fryer before starting to cook.

- Preheat your air fryer for 2 to 3 minutes before cooking.

- You can cook foods typically prepared in the oven in your air fryer. But because the air fryer is more condensed than a regular oven, it is recommended that recipes cut 25°F to 50°F off temperature and 20% off the typical cooking times.

- Avoid having foods stick to your air fryer basket by using nonstick cooking spray or cooking on parchment paper or foil. You can also get food to brown and crisp more easily by spraying occasionally with nonstick cooking spray during the cooking process.

- Don't overfill your basket. Each air fryer differs in its basket size. Cook foods in batches as needed.

- Use toothpicks to hold food in place. You may notice that light foods may blow around from the pressure of the fan. Just be sure to secure foods in the basket to prevent this.
- Check foods while cooking by opening the air fryer basket. This will not disturb cooking times. Once you return the basket, the cooking resumes.
- Experiment with cooking times of various foods. Test foods for doneness before consuming—check meats and poultry with a meat thermometer, and use a toothpick to test muffins and cupcakes.
- Use your air fryer to cook frozen foods, too! Frozen French fries, fish sticks, chicken nuggets, individual pizzas—these all work great. Just remember to reduce cooking temperatures and times.

estimated cooking temperatures/times*

FOOD	TEMPERATURE	TIMING
Vegetables (asparagus, broccoli, corn-on-the-cob, green beans, mushrooms, tomatoes)	390°F	6 to 10 min.
Vegetables (bell peppers, cauliflower, eggplant, onions, potatoes, zucchini)	390°F	10 to 15 min.
Chicken (bone-in)	370°F	20 to 25 min.
Chicken (boneless)	370°F	12 to 15 min.
Beef (ground beef)	370°F	15 to 17 min.
Beef (steaks, roasts)	390°F	10 to 15 min.
Pork	370°F	12 to 15 min.
Fish	390°F	10 to 12 min.
Frozen Foods	390°F	10 to 15 min.

*This is just a guide. All food varies in size, weight, and texture. Be sure to test your food for preferred doneness before consuming it. Also, some foods will need to be shaken or flipped to help distribute ingredients for proper cooking.

Make note of the temperatures and times that work best for you for continued success of your air fryer.

Enjoy and have fun!

APPETIZERS AND STARTERS

mozzarella sticks

¼ cup all-purpose flour

2 eggs

1 tablespoon water

1 cup plain dry bread crumbs

2 teaspoons Italian seasoning

½ teaspoon salt

½ teaspoon garlic powder

1 package (12 ounces) string cheese (12 sticks)

1 cup marinara or pizza sauce, heated

1 Place flour in shallow dish. Whisk eggs and water in another shallow dish. Combine bread crumbs, Italian seasoning, salt and garlic powder in third shallow dish.

2 Coat each piece of cheese with flour. Dip in egg mixture, letting excess drip back into dish. Roll in bread crumb mixture to coat. Dip again in egg mixture and roll again in bread crumb mixture. Place on baking sheet. Refrigerate until ready to cook.

3 Preheat air fryer to 370°F. Line basket with parchment paper; spray with nonstick cooking spray.

4 Cook in batches 8 to 10 minutes, flipping halfway through cooking, until golden brown. Serve with marinara sauce.

Makes 12 servings

green bean fries

dipping sauce

- ½ **cup light mayonnaise**
- ¼ **cup light sour cream**
- ¼ **cup low-fat buttermilk**
- ¼ **cup minced peeled cucumber**
- 1½ **teaspoons lemon juice**
- 1 **clove garlic**
- 1 **teaspoon wasabi powder**
- 1 **teaspoon prepared horseradish**
- ½ **teaspoon dried dill weed**
- ½ **teaspoon dried parsley flakes**
- ½ **teaspoon salt**
- ⅛ **teaspoon ground red pepper**

green bean fries

- 8 **ounces fresh green beans, trimmed**
- ⅓ **cup all-purpose flour**
- ⅓ **cup cornstarch**
- ½ **cup reduced-fat (2%) milk**
- 1 **egg**
- ¾ **cup plain dry bread crumbs**
- 1 **teaspoon salt**
- ½ **teaspoon onion powder**
- ¼ **teaspoon garlic powder**

1 For dipping sauce, combine mayonnaise, sour cream, buttermilk, cucumber, lemon juice, garlic, wasabi powder, horseradish, dill weed, parsley flakes, salt and red pepper in blender; blend until smooth. Refrigerate until ready to use.

2 For green bean fries, bring large saucepan of salted water to a boil. Add green beans; cook 4 minutes or until crisp-tender. Drain and run under cold running water to stop cooking.

3 Combine flour and cornstarch in large bowl. Whisk milk and egg in another large bowl. Combine bread crumbs, salt, onion powder and garlic powder in shallow dish. Place green beans in flour mixture; toss to coat. Working in batches, coat beans with egg mixture, letting excess drain back into bowl. Roll green beans in bread crumb mixture to coat.

4 Preheat air fryer to 390°F. Cook in batches 6 to 8 minutes, shaking occasionally during cooking, until golden brown. Serve warm with dipping sauce.

Makes 6 servings

buffalo—style oyster mushrooms

1½ teaspoons paprika

1½ teaspoons poultry seasoning

1½ teaspoons celery seed

2 teaspoons garlic powder

½ teaspoon chili powder

1 teaspoon onion powder

½ teaspoon ground sage

½ teaspoon dried thyme

¾ cup panko bread crumbs

½ cup all-purpose flour

1 cup buttermilk

2 tablespoons hot pepper sauce

2 cups (about 4 ounces) oyster mushrooms

Blue cheese dressing and celery sticks

1 Combine paprika, poultry seasoning, celery seed, garlic powder, chili powder, onion powder, sage, thyme and panko in medium bowl. Set aside.

2 Place flour in large bowl; slowly whisk buttermilk and hot pepper sauce into flour until combined and no longer lumpy.

3 Using a fork, coat mushrooms with buttermilk mixture. Dip into spice mixture, coating thoroughly. Spray mushrooms with nonstick cooking spray.

4 Preheat air fryer to 390°F. Line basket with parchment paper.

5 Cook mushrooms 6 to 8 minutes or until browned. Serve with dressing and celery sticks.

Makes 2 to 4 servings

sweet cocktail meatballs

meatballs

- 1 pound ground beef
- ⅔ cup instant oats
- ½ cup crushed butter crackers
- 1 egg
- 1 teaspoon dry onion flakes
- 1 teaspoon minced garlic
- 1 teaspoon honey
- ¼ teaspoon black pepper

sauce

- ⅓ cup packed brown sugar
- ¼ cup honey
- ¼ cup orange marmalade
- 1 teaspoon cornstarch (optional)
- 1 tablespoon soy sauce
- 1 tablespoon hot pepper sauce

1 For meatballs, combine beef, oats, cracker crumbs, egg, onion flakes, garlic, 1 teaspoon honey and black pepper in large bowl; mix well. Shape mixture into 1-inch balls; place on baking sheet. Refrigerate at least 30 minutes.

2 For sauce, combine brown sugar, ¼ cup honey, marmalade, cornstarch, if desired for thicker sauce, soy sauce and hot pepper sauce in medium saucepan. Heat over medium heat, stirring occasionally, until mixture begins to thicken. Reduce heat to low; keep warm.

3 Preheat air fryer to 390°F. Line basket with parchment paper.

4 Cook meatballs 8 to 10 minutes or until cooked through and browned. Transfer meatballs to serving bowl. Pour sauce over meatballs to serve.

Makes 1½ dozen meatballs

pepper pizza poppers

4 to 6 mini sweet bell peppers, red, orange and yellow

½ cup marinara sauce

½ cup (2 ounces) shredded mozzarella cheese

Sliced olives, mushrooms, mini pepperoni slices (optional)

1 teaspoon chopped fresh oregano

1 Preheat air fryer to 370°F.

2 Slice peppers in half horizontally, removing seeds, but keeping stem intact.

3 Equally divide sauce among pepper halves. Top with cheese, olives, mushrooms or pepperoni, as desired. Sprinkle with oregano.

4 Cook 5 to 7 minutes or until cheese is melted and begins to brown.

Makes 4 to 6 servings

crispy mushrooms

½ **cup all-purpose flour**

½ **cup garlic and herb-flavored bread crumbs**

½ **cup grated Parmesan cheese**

½ **teaspoon paprika**

½ **teaspoon salt**

¼ **teaspoon black pepper**

2 **eggs**

1 **teaspoon water**

1 **package (8 ounces) whole mushrooms**

garlic mayonnaise

½ **cup mayonnaise**

2 **teaspoons minced garlic**

1 **teaspoon lemon juice**

Fresh chopped parsley (optional)

1 Combine flour, bread crumbs, Parmesan cheese, paprika, salt and pepper in medium bowl. Whisk eggs and water in separate bowl.

2 Preheat air fryer to 370°F. Line basket with parchment paper.

3 Using a fork, dip mushrooms into egg mixture, allowing excess to drip back into bowl. Coat with bread crumb mixture, coating thoroughly. Spray mushrooms with nonstick cooking spray.

4 Cook in batches 6 to 8 minutes or until golden brown, spraying with cooking spray halfway through cooking.

5 Prepare Garlic Mayonnaise. Combine mayonnaise, garlic and lemon juice in small bowl; mix well. Sprinkle with parsley, if desired. Serve mushrooms with Garlic Mayonnaise.

Makes 4 servings

burger bites

1 **pound lean ground beef**

2 **tablespoons Dijon mustard**

½ **teaspoon minced onion**

½ **teaspoon salt**

¼ **teaspoon black pepper**

Cherry tomatoes

Butter lettuce

Pickle slices

Mini skewers or picks

Dipping sauce, ketchup, mayonnaise or mustard for dipping

1 Combine beef, mustard, minced onion, salt and pepper in medium bowl. Using your hands, form into about 12 to 16 balls.

2 Preheat air fryer to 390°F. Line basket with parchment paper.

3 Cook, in batches, 10 to 12 minutes or until meatballs test done. Remove to plate. Cool slightly.

4 Thread tomatoes, lettuce, pickles and burger bites on skewer. Serve with dipping sauce as desired.

variation

Add sliced cheese or a fresh mozzarella ball, if desired.

Makes 6 to 8 servings

loaded tater tots

1 package (16 ounces) frozen bite-sized potato nuggets (tater tots)

½ cup (2 ounces) shredded Cheddar cheese

2 slices bacon, crisp-cooked and crumbled* *or* 2 tablespoons bacon bits

2 tablespoons sour cream

2 green onions, chopped

Chopped avocado (optional)

*Cook bacon in preheated 390°F air fryer 6 to 8 minutes or until crispy. Remove to paper towel-lined plate. Cool completely.

1 Preheat air fryer to 390°F.

2 Cook potatoes in single layer 6 to 8 minutes, shaking occasionally during cooking. Remove to baking dish that fits inside air fryer.

3 Sprinkle cheese and bacon over potatoes. Cook 2 to 3 minutes or until cheese is melted.

4 Drizzle with sour cream; sprinkle with green onions and avocado, if desired. Serve immediately.

Makes 3 to 4 servings

mini pepper nachos

- 1 cup frozen corn, thawed
- 1 can (about 15 ounces) black beans, rinsed and drained
- ½ cup chopped tomatoes
- ½ teaspoon salt
- 20 mini sweet peppers, assorted colors, cut in half lengthwise and seeded
- ½ cup (2 ounces) shredded Mexican-style taco cheese
- ½ cup sour cream (optional)
- 1 small avocado, chopped (optional)
- 2 tablespoons chopped green onion or cilantro (optional)

1 Combine corn, beans, tomatoes and salt in medium bowl. Fill peppers with about 1 tablespoon mixture. Sprinkle with cheese.

2 Preheat air fryer to 370°F. Line basket with foil. Cook 5 to 7 minutes or until cheese is lightly browned and melted. Remove to serving plate.

3 Top with sour cream, avocado and green onion, if desired.

Makes 40 pepper halves (2 per serving)

caprese portobellos

2 tablespoons butter

½ teaspoon minced garlic

1 teaspoon dried parsley flakes

4 portobello mushrooms, stems removed

1 cup (4 ounces) shredded part-skim mozzarella cheese

1 cup cherry or grape tomatoes, thinly sliced

2 tablespoons fresh basil, thinly sliced

Balsamic glaze

1 Combine butter, garlic and parsley flakes in small microwavable dish. Microwave on LOW (30%) 30 seconds or until melted.

2 Wash mushrooms thoroughly; dry on paper towels. Brush both sides of mushrooms with butter mixture.

3 Preheat air fryer to 390°F. Spray basket with nonstick cooking spray.

4 Fill mushroom caps with about ¼ cup cheese each. Top with tomatoes. Cook 5 to 7 minutes or until cheese is melted and lightly browned. Top with basil.

5 Drizzle with balsamic glaze before serving.

Makes 4 servings

parmesan pickle chips

4 **large whole dill pickles**
½ **cup all-purpose flour**
½ **teaspoon salt**
2 **eggs**
½ **cup panko bread crumbs**
2 **tablespoons grated
    Parmesan cheese**
½ **cup garlic aioli mayonnaise
    or ranch dressing**

1 Line baking sheet with paper towels. Slice pickles diagonally into ¼-inch slices; place on prepared baking sheet. Pat dry on top with paper towels to remove any moisture from pickles.

2 Combine flour and salt in shallow dish. Beat eggs in another shallow dish. Combine panko and Parmesan cheese in third shallow dish.

3 Coat pickles in flour. Dip in eggs, letting excess drip back into dish, then coat evenly with panko mixture.

4 Preheat air fryer to 390°F. Cook in batches 8 to 10 minutes or until golden brown. Remove carefully. Serve with aioli or dressing.

Makes 8 servings

toasted ravioli

1 cup all-purpose flour

2 eggs

¼ cup water

1 cup plain dry bread crumbs

1 teaspoon Italian seasoning

¾ teaspoon garlic powder

¼ teaspoon salt

½ cup grated Parmesan cheese

2 tablespoons finely chopped fresh parsley (optional)

1 package (10 ounces) cheese or meat ravioli, thawed if frozen

½ cup pasta sauce, heated

1 Place flour in shallow dish. Whisk eggs and water in another shallow dish. Combine bread crumbs, Italian seasoning, garlic powder and salt in third shallow dish. Combine Parmesan cheese and parsley, if desired, in large bowl.

2 Coat ravioli with flour. Dip in egg mixture, letting excess drip back into dish. Roll in bread crumb mixture to coat. Spray with nonstick cooking spray.

3 Preheat air fryer to 390°F. Poke holes in ravioli with toothpick.

4 Cook in batches 5 to 6 minutes, turning once, until golden brown. Add to bowl with cheese; toss to coat. Serve warm with sauce.

Makes 6 servings

baked salami

1 **all-beef kosher salami (14 to 16 ounces)**

½ **cup apricot preserves**

1 **tablespoon hot pepper sauce**

2 **tablespoons packed brown sugar**

Bread slices

1 Peel off plastic wrap of salami. Cut 12 crosswise (½-inch-deep) slits across top. Place, cut side up, in small dish that fits inside air fryer.

2 Combine preserves, hot pepper sauce and brown sugar in small bowl; stir well. Spoon sauce over top.

3 Preheat air fryer to 370°F. Cook 8 to 10 minutes or until juicy and dark brown, spooning sauce over salami occasionally during cooking.

4 Cut salami into thin slices; toss with sauce. Serve on bread.

extras

Serve with slices of challah bread or cocktail rye.

Makes 5 servings

BREAKFAST

breakfast flats

1 package (about 14 ounces) refrigerated pizza dough

1½ cups (6 ounces) shredded Cheddar cheese

8 slices bacon, crisp-cooked and diced (optional)

4 eggs, fried

Kosher salt and black pepper (optional)

1 Divide pizza dough into 4 equal portions. Roll out on lightly floured surface into rectangles roughly 8½×4 inches. Top each evenly with cheese and bacon, if desired.

2 Preheat air fryer to 370°F. Line basket with parchment paper.

3 Cook in batches 5 to 7 minutes or until crust is golden brown and crisp and cheese is melted.

4 Top baked flats with fried egg; season with salt and pepper, if desired. Serve warm.

Makes 4 servings

ricotta pancakes

- 1 package (15 ounces) whole milk ricotta cheese
- 1 egg
- ½ teaspoon vanilla
- ¼ cup granulated sugar
- 1 cup all-purpose flour, divided
- ¼ teaspoon baking powder
- ½ cup seedless raspberry jam
- Powdered sugar
- Fresh raspberries (optional)

1 Combine ricotta cheese and egg in large bowl; mix well. Add vanilla; stir. Add granulated sugar, ¾ cup flour and baking powder. Mix well. Put remaining ¼ cup flour in medium bowl.

2 Scoop about ¼ to ½ cup mixture into a ball. Add to bowl with flour; coat well. Flatten into pancake about ½ inch thick. Repeat with remaining batter. Spray with nonstick cooking spray.

3 Preheat air fryer to 370°F. Line basket with parchment paper.

4 Cook in batches 14 to 16 minutes or until lightly browned, flipping and spraying with cooking spray after 10 minutes.

5 Place raspberry jam in small microwavable bowl; microwave on HIGH 30 seconds or until melted. Drizzle over warm pancakes. Sprinkle with powdered sugar. Garnish with raspberries, if desired.

Makes 8 to 10 pancakes

strawberry banana french toast

1 cup sliced fresh strawberries (about 8 medium)

2 teaspoons granulated sugar

2 eggs

½ cup milk

3 tablespoons all-purpose flour

1 teaspoon vanilla

⅛ teaspoon salt

4 slices (1 inch thick) egg bread or country bread

1 banana, cut into ¼-inch slices

Whipped cream and powdered sugar (optional)

Maple syrup

1 Combine strawberries and granulated sugar in small bowl; toss to coat. Set aside while preparing French toast.

2 Whisk eggs, milk, flour, vanilla and salt in shallow bowl or pie plate until well blended. Working with 2 slices at a time, dip bread into egg mixture, turning to coat completely; let excess drip off.

3 Preheat air fryer to 370°F. Cook 8 to 10 minutes or until golden brown. Repeat with remaining bread slices.

4 Top each serving with strawberry mixture and banana slices. Garnish with whipped cream and powdered sugar, if desired. Serve with maple syrup.

Makes 2 servings

omelet scramble

2 large eggs

2 tablespoons milk

¼ teaspoon salt

⅛ teaspoon black pepper

2 tablespoons chopped red and/or green bell pepper

2 tablespoons chopped onion

¼ cup (1 ounce) shredded Cheddar cheese, divided

1 Spray 6×3-inch baking dish or 2 small ramekins* with nonstick cooking spray.

2 Whisk eggs, milk, salt and black pepper in medium bowl. Add bell pepper, onion and 2 tablespoons cheese. Pour into prepared dish.

3 Preheat air fryer to 350°F. Cook 10 to 12 minutes, slightly breaking up eggs after 5 minutes. Top with remaining cheese.

Depending on the size of your air fryer, you may need to modify the size of the baking dish.

Makes 2 servings

baked apple pancake

3 tablespoons butter

3 medium Granny Smith apples (about 1¼ pounds), peeled and cut into ¼-inch slices

½ cup packed dark brown sugar

1½ teaspoons ground cinnamon

½ teaspoon plus pinch of salt, divided

4 eggs

⅓ cup whipping cream

⅓ cup milk

2 tablespoons granulated sugar

½ teaspoon vanilla

⅔ cup all-purpose flour

1 Melt butter in 8-inch nonstick skillet over medium heat. Add apples, brown sugar, cinnamon and pinch of salt; cook 8 minutes or until apples begin to soften, stirring occasionally. Cool 30 minutes. Spray 8-inch pie pan* with nonstick cooking spray. Spread apples in even layer in pie pan.

2 Whisk eggs in large bowl until foamy. Add cream, milk, granulated sugar, vanilla and remaining ½ teaspoon salt; whisk until blended. Sift flour into egg mixture; whisk until batter is well blended and smooth. Set aside 15 minutes.

3 Stir batter. Pour evenly over apple mixture. Preheat air fryer to 370°F.

4 Cook 8 to 10 minutes or until top is golden brown and pancake is loose around edge. Cool 1 minute; loosen edge of pancake with spatula, if necessary. Place large serving plate or cutting board on top of pie pan and invert pancake onto plate. Serve warm.

If your air fryer is on the smaller side, use 2 smaller baking dishes or ramekins.

Makes 2 to 4 servings

breakfast pepperoni flatbread

1 flatbread

½ cup (2 ounces) shredded mozzarella cheese

1 plum tomato, diced

12 slices turkey pepperoni, cut into quarters

1 teaspoon grated Parmesan cheese

¼ cup chopped fresh basil

1 Place flatbread on parchment paper. Sprinkle with mozzarella cheese, tomato, pepperoni and Parmesan cheese.

2 Preheat air fryer to 370°F.

3 Cook 3 to 5 minutes or until cheese is melted. Sprinkle with basil. Cool slightly before cutting.

Makes 2 servings

broiled grapefruit your way

1 large pink grapefruit

2 teaspoons honey

2 teaspoons packed brown sugar

1 Cut grapefruit in half horizontally. Use a sharp knife to cut around edges and sections of grapefruit where the rind meets the fruit.

2 Drizzle each half with honey; sprinkle with brown sugar.

3 Preheat air fryer to 400°F. Cook 5 to 7 minutes or until lightly browned and bubbly.

variation

Sprinkle grapefruit with cinnamon-sugar mixture or toasted coconut instead of honey and brown sugar.

Makes 2 servings

biscuit doughnuts

1 package (about 16 ounces) refrigerated jumbo biscuit dough (8 biscuits)

¼ cup honey

1 teaspoon chopped pistachio nuts

1 Separate dough into 8 portions. Using hands, create a hole in the middle to create doughnut shape.

2 Preheat air fryer to 370°F.

3 Cook in batches 7 to 8 minutes or until golden brown.

4 Drizzle warm doughnuts with honey. Sprinkle with pistachios.

variation

For cinnamon-sugar coating, combine ¼ cup sugar and 1 teaspoon ground cinnamon in small bowl. Dip warm doughnuts in cinnamon-sugar.

Makes 8 doughnuts

LIGHT MEALS

salmon croquettes

1 can (14¾ ounces) pink salmon, drained and flaked

½ cup mashed potatoes*

1 egg, beaten

3 tablespoons diced red bell pepper

2 tablespoons sliced green onion

1 tablespoon chopped fresh parsley

½ cup seasoned dry bread crumbs

Use mashed potatoes that are freshly made, leftover, or potatoes made from instant potatoes.

1 Combine salmon, potatoes, egg, bell pepper, green onion and parsley in medium bowl; mix well.

2 Place bread crumbs on medium plate. Shape salmon mixture into 10 croquettes about 3 inches long by 1 inch wide. Roll croquettes in bread crumbs to coat. Place on baking sheet. Refrigerate 15 to 20 minutes or until firm.

3 Preheat air fryer to 350°F. Cook in batches 6 to 8 minutes or until browned. Serve immediately.

Makes 5 servings (2 per serving)

pizza sandwich

1 loaf (12 ounces) focaccia

½ cup pizza sauce

20 slices pepperoni

8 slices (1 ounce each) mozzarella cheese

1 can (2¼ ounces) sliced mushrooms, drained

Red pepper flakes (optional)

Olive oil

1 Cut focaccia horizontally in half.* Spread cut sides of both halves with pizza sauce. Layer bottom half with pepperoni, cheese and mushrooms; sprinkle with red pepper flakes, if desired. Cover with top half of focaccia. Brush sandwich lightly with oil.

2 Preheat air fryer to 370°F.

3 Cook 3 to 5 minutes or until cheese melts and bread is golden brown. Cut into wedges to serve.

Depending on the size of your air fryer, you may need to cut the focaccia vertically in half to fit.

note

Focaccia can be found in the bakery section of most supermarkets. It is often available in different flavors, such as tomato, herb, cheese or onion.

Makes 4 to 6 servings

eggplant pizzas

1 **large egg**

1 **tablespoon water**

¾ **cup Italian-seasoned dry bread crumbs**

1 **medium eggplant, unpeeled and sliced into ½-inch rounds**

½ **cup marinara sauce**

½ **cup (2 ounces) shredded mozzarella cheese**

Chopped fresh basil

1 Beat egg and water in shallow dish. Place bread crumbs in another shallow dish. Dip eggplant in egg, letting excess drip back into dish. Dredge in bread crumbs, pressing gently to adhere. Spray with nonstick cooking spray.

2 Preheat air fryer to 370°F. Line basket with foil.

3 Cook in batches 10 to 12 minutes or until slightly tender and golden brown.

4 Place about 1 tablespoon marinara sauce on top of each eggplant slice. Top each with about 1 tablespoon cheese. Return to air fryer; cook 3 to 5 minutes or until cheese is melted and golden brown.

5 Sprinkle with basil.

note

Add bell peppers, sliced tomatoes, olives or any other favorite topping.

Makes 4 servings (2 pizzas each)

chicken waldorf salad

dressing

- ⅓ cup balsamic vinegar
- 2 tablespoons Dijon mustard
- 2 teaspoons minced garlic
- ½ teaspoon salt
- ¼ teaspoon black pepper
- ⅔ cup extra virgin olive oil

salad

- 4 boneless skinless chicken breasts (about 4 ounces each)
- Salt and black pepper (optional)
- 8 cups mixed greens
- 1 large Granny Smith apple, cut into ½-inch pieces
- ⅔ cup diced celery
- ⅔ cup halved red seedless grapes
- ½ cup candied walnuts*
- ½ cup crumbled blue cheese

Candied or glazed walnuts may be found in the produce section of the supermarket with other salad toppings, or they may be found in the snack aisle.

1 For dressing, combine vinegar, mustard, garlic, ½ teaspoon salt and ¼ teaspoon pepper in medium bowl; mix well. Slowly add oil, whisking until well blended.

2 Preheat air fryer to 370°F. Spray basket with nonstick cooking spray. Season chicken with salt and pepper, if desired. Cook 12 to 15 minutes or until no longer pink in center and cooked throughout (165°F). Cool slightly; slice chicken.

3 For salad, combine mixed greens, apple, celery and grapes in large bowl. Add half of dressing; toss to coat. Top with chicken, walnuts and cheese; drizzle with additional dressing.

Makes 4 servings

nashville-style hot chicken sandwich

2 tablespoons hot pepper sauce, divided

2 tablespoons dill pickle juice, divided

1 teaspoon salt, divided

2 pounds chicken breast strips or tenders

1 cup all-purpose flour

½ teaspoon black pepper

1 egg

½ cup buttermilk

¼ cup olive oil

1 tablespoon red pepper flakes

1 tablespoon packed brown sugar

½ teaspoon paprika

½ teaspoon chili powder

¼ teaspoon garlic powder

4 to 6 Brioche buns, toasted

White Cheddar cheese slices (optional)

Sweet coleslaw and dill pickle slices

1 Combine 1 tablespoon hot pepper sauce, 1 tablespoon pickle juice and ½ teaspoon salt in large resealable food storage bag. Add chicken; seal and turn to coat. Refrigerate 1 hour to overnight.

2 Combine flour, remaining ½ teaspoon salt and black pepper in shallow dish. Whisk egg, buttermilk, remaining 1 tablespoon hot pepper sauce and remaining 1 tablespoon pickle juice in another shallow dish. Remove chicken from marinade; discard marinade. Coat chicken with flour mixture, then dip in egg mixture and again in flour mixture.

3 Preheat air fryer to 390°F. Spray basket with nonstick cooking spray. Cook chicken in batches 18 to 20 minutes or until no longer pink in center and cooked throughout (165°F), turning chicken halfway through cooking and spraying occasionally with cooking spray. Remove chicken to large platter.

4 Combine oil, red pepper flakes, brown sugar, paprika, chili powder and garlic powder in small bowl; pour over chicken.

5 Serve chicken on toasted bun with cheese, if desired, coleslaw and pickles.

Makes 4 to 6 servings

shrimp and spinach salad

3 to 4 slices bacon

dressing

¼ cup red wine vinegar

½ teaspoon cornstarch

¼ cup olive oil

¼ cup sugar

¼ teaspoon salt

¼ teaspoon black pepper

¼ teaspoon liquid smoke

shrimp

2 teaspoons black pepper

1 teaspoon salt

1 teaspoon garlic powder

½ teaspoon sugar

½ teaspoon onion powder

½ teaspoon ground sage

½ teaspoon paprika

20 to 24 large raw shrimp, peeled and deveined

salad

8 cups packed torn stemmed spinach

1 tomato, diced

½ red onion, thinly sliced

½ cup sliced roasted red peppers

1 Preheat air fryer to 400°F. Cook bacon 8 to 10 minutes or until crisp. Drain on paper towel-lined plate. Crumble bacon; set aside.

2 For dressing, stir vinegar into cornstarch in small bowl until smooth. Whisk in ¼ cup oil, ¼ cup sugar, ¼ teaspoon salt, ¼ teaspoon black pepper and liquid smoke until well blended.

3 For shrimp, combine 2 teaspoons black pepper, 1 teaspoon salt, garlic powder, ½ teaspoon sugar, onion powder, sage and paprika in medium bowl; mix well. Add shrimp; toss to coat.

4 Preheat air fryer to 390°F. Cook shrimp 6 to 8 minutes or until shrimp is pink and opaque.

5 For salad, combine spinach, tomato, onion and roasted peppers in large bowl. Add two thirds of dressing; toss to coat. Top with shrimp and crumbled bacon; serve with remaining dressing.

Makes 4 servings

mushroom po-boys

Remoulade Sauce
(recipe follows)*

1 cup buttermilk

1 tablespoon hot pepper
   sauce

1¼ cups all-purpose flour

1 teaspoon salt

1 teaspoon smoked paprika

¼ teaspoon onion powder

¼ teaspoon black pepper

1 package (4 ounces) sliced
   shiitake mushrooms

1 package (3 ounces)
   oyster mushrooms, cut
   into 2-inch or bite-size
   pieces

1 loaf French bread, ends
   trimmed, cut into
   4 pieces and split

   Sliced fresh tomatoes and
   finely shredded iceberg
   lettuce

*Or substitute plain
mayonnaise for serving.*

1 Prepare Remoulade Sauce; cover and refrigerate until ready to use.

2 Combine buttermilk and 1 tablespoon hot pepper sauce in medium bowl. Whisk flour, salt, paprika, onion powder and black pepper in another medium bowl. Dip mushroom pieces, a few at a time, in buttermilk mixture; roll in flour mixture to coat. Dip again in buttermilk mixture and roll in flour mixture; place on plate. Repeat until all mushrooms are coated.

3 Preheat air fryer to 370°F. Line basket with parchment paper; spray with nonstick cooking spray. Working in batches if necessary, arrange mushrooms in single layer in basket; spray tops with cooking spray. Cook 8 to 10 minutes or until coating is crisp and browned.

4 Serve mushrooms on bread with tomatoes, lettuce and Remoulade sauce.

remoulade sauce

Combine ½ cup mayonnaise, 2 tablespoons Dijon or coarse grain mustard, 1 tablespoon lemon juice, 1 clove garlic, minced, and ½ teaspoon hot pepper sauce in small bowl.

Makes 4 servings

turkey dinner quesadilla

1 **(10- to 12-inch) flour tortilla**

2 **slices deli turkey**

2 **slices (1 ounce each) Swiss cheese**

2 **tablespoons whole berry cranberry sauce**

¼ **cup baby spinach**

1 Preheat air fryer to 370°F.

2 Lay tortilla on flat surface. Cut one slit from outer edge of tortilla to center (as seen in photo below).

3 Place turkey slices, cheese slices, cranberry sauce and spinach in each of the 4 quadrants. Beginning with the cut edge, fold the tortilla in quarters, covering each quadrant until you have the entire quesadilla folded into one large triangle. Spray outside of quesadilla with nonstick cooking spray.

4 Cook 3 to 5 minutes or until tortilla browns and begins to get crispy.

Makes 1 serving

strawberry poppy seed chicken salad

dressing

- ¼ cup white wine vinegar
- 2 tablespoons orange juice
- 1 tablespoon sugar
- 2 teaspoons poppy seeds
- 1½ teaspoons Dijon mustard
- ½ teaspoon salt
- ½ teaspoon minced dried onion
- ½ cup vegetable oil

salad

- 4 boneless skinless chicken breasts (about 4 ounces each)

  Salt and black pepper (optional)
- 8 cups romaine lettuce
- ¾ cup fresh pineapple chunks
- ¾ cup sliced fresh strawberries
- ¾ cup fresh blueberries
- 1 navel orange, peeled and sectioned *or* 1 can (11 ounces) mandarin oranges, drained
- ¼ cup chopped toasted pecans*

  To toast nuts, cook in preheated 325°F parchment-lined air fryer 3 to 4 minutes or until golden brown.

1 For dressing, combine vinegar, orange juice, sugar, poppy seeds, mustard, ½ teaspoon salt and dried onion in small bowl; mix well. Whisk in oil in thin, steady stream until well blended.

2 Preheat air fryer to 370°F. Spray basket with nonstick cooking spray. Season chicken with salt and pepper, if desired. Cook 12 to 15 minutes or until no longer pink and cooked throughout (165°F). Cool slightly; slice chicken.

3 For salad, combine lettuce and two thirds of dressing in large bowl; toss gently to coat. Divide salad among 4 plates, top with chicken, pineapple, strawberries, blueberries, oranges and pecans. Serve with remaining dressing.

Makes 4 servings

classic patty melts

4 tablespoons (½ stick) butter, divided and melted

2 large yellow onions, thinly sliced

¾ teaspoon plus pinch of salt, divided

1 pound ground chuck (80% lean)

½ teaspoon garlic powder

½ teaspoon onion powder

¼ teaspoon black pepper

8 slices marble rye bread

½ cup Thousand Island dressing

8 slices (1 ounce each) deli American or Swiss cheese

1 Preheat air fryer to 370°F.

2 Combine 2 tablespoons melted butter, onions and pinch of salt in large skillet; cook 12 to 15 minutes, shaking and tossing occasionally, until onions are very soft and golden brown. Remove to bowl.

3 Combine beef, remaining ¾ teaspoon salt, garlic powder, onion powder and pepper in medium bowl; mix gently. Shape into 4 (¼- to ½-inch thick) patties.

4 Cook patties 12 to 14 minutes, flipping halfway through cooking, until browned and cooked throughout (160°F).

5 Brush remaining 2 tablespoons melted butter on outside of each bread slice. Spread dressing on inside of bread slices. Layer 4 bread slices with cheese slice, patty, caramelized onions, another cheese slice and remaining bread slices.

6 Cook 2 to 4 minutes or until bread is golden brown and cheese is melted, flipping halfway through cooking.

Makes 4 servings

chicken parmesan sliders

4 boneless skinless chicken breasts (4 to 6 ounces each)

¼ cup all-purpose flour

2 eggs

1 tablespoon water

1 cup Italian-seasoned dry bread crumbs

½ cup grated Parmesan cheese

Salt and black pepper

12 slider buns (about 3 inches), split

¾ cup marinara sauce

6 tablespoons Alfredo sauce

6 slices (1 ounce each) mozzarella cheese, cut into halves

6 tablespoons prepared pesto

2 tablespoons butter, melted

¼ teaspoon garlic powder

1 Pound chicken to ½-inch thickness between 2 sheets of waxed paper or plastic wrap with rolling pin or meat mallet. Cut each chicken breast crosswise into 3 pieces about the size of slider buns.

2 Place flour in shallow dish. Beat eggs and water in second shallow dish. Combine bread crumbs and Parmesan cheese in third shallow dish. Season flour and egg mixtures with pinch of salt and pepper. Coat chicken pieces lightly with flour, shaking off excess. Dip in egg mixture, coating completely; roll in bread crumb mixture to coat. Place on large plate; let stand 10 minutes.

3 Preheat air fryer to 370°F. Line basket with foil.

4 Cook chicken in batches, if necessary, 10 to 12 minutes, flipping halfway through cooking or until golden brown and cooked through (165°F). Remove chicken.

5 Arrange slider buns on foil-lined basket with bottoms cut sides up and tops cut sides down. Spread 1 tablespoon marinara sauce over each bottom bun; top with piece of chicken. Spread ½ tablespoon Alfredo sauce over chicken; top with half slice of mozzarella. Spread ½ tablespoon pesto over cheese; cover with top buns.

6 Combine butter and garlic powder in small bowl; brush mixture over bun tops. Cook 1 to 2 minutes or until cheese is melted and top buns are lightly browned.

Makes 12 sliders

hearty veggie sandwich

1 pound cremini mushrooms, stemmed and thinly sliced (⅛-inch slices)

2 teapoons olive oil, divided

¾ teaspoon salt, divided

¼ teaspoon black pepper

1 medium zucchini, diced (¼-inch pieces, about 2 cups)

3 tablespoons butter, softened

8 slices artisan whole grain bread

¼ cup prepared pesto

¼ cup mayonnaise

2 cups packed baby spinach

4 slices (1 ounce each) mozzarella cheese

1 Preheat air fryer to 370°F. Combine mushrooms, 1 teaspoon oil, ½ teaspoon salt and pepper in medium bowl; toss to coat. Cook 6 to 8 minutes or until mushrooms are dark brown and dry, shaking occasionally. Remove to medium bowl.

2 Toss remaining 1 teaspoon oil, zucchini and remaining ¼ teaspoon salt in small bowl. Cook 2 to 4 minutes or until zucchini is tender and lightly browned. Remove to bowl.

3 Spread butter on one side of each bread slice. Turn over slices. Spread pesto on 4 bread slices; spread mayonnaise on remaining 4 slices. Top pesto-covered slices evenly with mushrooms; layer with spinach, zucchini and cheese. Top with remaining bread slices, mayonnaise side down.

4 Cook 2 to 4 minutes or until bread is toasted, spinach is slightly wilted and cheese is beginning to melt. Serve immediately.

Makes 4 servings

hawaiian pizza rolls

2 tablespoons cornmeal, divided

1 package (about 14 ounces) refrigerated pizza dough

6 ounces thinly sliced Canadian bacon

⅓ cup crushed pineapple, drained

⅓ cup pizza sauce, plus additional for serving

3 pieces (1 ounce each) string cheese

1 Sprinkle 1 tablespoon cornmeal on cutting board. Roll out dough to 16½×11-inch rectangle. Sprinkle with remaining 1 tablespoon cornmeal. Cut into 6 squares. Top each square with bacon, pineapple and pizza sauce.

2 Cut each piece of string cheese in half; place 1 piece of cheese in center of each square. Bring up two opposite sides of each square and crimp ends of each roll to seal.

3 Preheat air fryer to 370°F. Spray basket with nonstick cooking spray.

4 Cook, seam side down, in batches 6 to 8 minutes or until golden brown. Serve warm at room temperature or chilled.

tip

Serve extra prepared pizza sauce on the side for dipping.

Makes 6 servings

one-bite burgers

1 package (11 ounces) refrigerated breadstick dough (12 breadsticks)

1 pound ground beef

2 teaspoons hamburger seasoning mix*

9 slices Cheddar or American cheese, quartered (optional)

36 round dill pickle slices

Ketchup and mustard

Or you can season with garlic powder, onion powder, chili powder, salt and/or black pepper.

1 Preheat air fryer to 370°F. Separate dough into 12 breadsticks; cut each breadstick into 3 equal pieces. Working with one piece at a time, tuck ends under to meet at center, pressing to seal and form very small bun about 1½ inches in diameter and ½ inch high.

2 Place buns seam side down in basket.** Cook 8 to 10 minutes or until golden brown. Remove to wire racks.

3 Meanwhile, gently mix beef and seasoning mix in large bowl. Shape beef mixture into 36 patties, using about 2 teaspoons beef per patty.

4 Preheat air fryer to 390°F. Line basket with parchment paper. Cook patties 6 to 8 minutes or until cooked through (160°F), flipping once. Top with cheese slice, if desired.

5 Split buns in half crosswise. Place burgers on bottom of buns. Top with pickle slices, small dollops of ketchup and mustard and tops of buns.

**If you like, spray buns lightly with nonstick cooking spray and add a sprinkle of sesame seeds before cooking.

Makes 36 mini burgers

DINNER

buttermilk air-fried chicken

1 **cut-up whole chicken (2½ to 3 pounds)**

1 **cup buttermilk**

¾ **cup all-purpose flour**

½ **teaspoon salt**

½ **teaspoon ground red pepper**

¼ **teaspoon garlic powder**

2 **cups plain dry bread crumbs**

1 Place chicken pieces in large resealable food storage bag. Pour buttermilk over chicken. Close and refrigerate; let marinate at least 2 hours.

2 Combine flour, salt, red pepper and garlic powder in large shallow dish. Place bread crumbs in another shallow dish.

3 Preheat air fryer to 370°F. Spray basket with nonstick cooking spray.

4 Remove chicken pieces from buttermilk; coat with flour mixture then coat in bread crumbs. Spray chicken with cooking spray. Cook in batches 20 to 25 minutes or until brown and crisp on all sides and cooked through (165°F). Serve warm.

Makes 4 servings

beef taquitos

¾ **pound ground beef**

¼ **cup chopped onion**

1 **tablespoon taco seasoning mix**

6 **corn tortillas**

⅓ **cup shredded Cheddar cheese, plus additional for topping**

Salsa, sour cream and guacamole (optional)

1 Cook beef and onion in large skillet over medium-high heat 6 to 8 minutes or until browned, stirring to break up meat. Drain fat. Stir in taco seasoning mix.

2 Spoon about 2 tablespoons beef mixture in center of each tortilla. Top with about 1 tablespoon cheese. Roll up; secure with toothpicks. Spray with nonstick cooking spray.

3 Preheat air fryer to 370°F. Cook in single layer 3 to 4 minutes or until tortilla is browned and crispy.

4 Remove toothpicks before serving. Top with salsa, sour cream, guacamole and/or additional cheese.

substitution tip

Try preparing taquitos with cooked chicken or pork and other types of cheese as well.

Makes 6 servings

parmesan-crusted chicken

4 to 6 boneless skinless chicken breasts (about 4 ounces each)

Salt and black pepper (optional)

1¼ cups Italian salad dressing

½ cup grated Parmesan cheese

½ cup finely shredded Provolone cheese

¼ cup buttermilk ranch salad dressing

4 tablespoons (½ stick) butter, melted

1 teaspoon minced garlic

¾ cup panko bread crumbs

1 Pound chicken to ½- to ¾-inch thickness between 2 sheets of waxed paper or plastic wrap with rolling pin or meat mallet. Season chicken with salt and pepper, if desired; place in large resealable food storage bag. Pour Italian dressing over chicken. Marinate in refrigerator at least 30 minutes.

2 Preheat air fryer to 370°F. Remove chicken from marinade. Cook 12 to 15 minutes, turning halfway through cooking, until chicken is no longer pink in center and cooked throughout (165°F).

3 Combine Parmesan cheese, Provolone, ranch dressing, butter and garlic in large microwavable bowl. Microwave 30 seconds; stir. Add panko; mix to combine. Spread mixture over chicken.

4 Preheat air fryer to 390°F. Cook 2 to 3 minutes or until cheese is melted and topping is browned.

serving suggestion

Serve with fresh steamed broccoli.

Makes 4 to 6 servings

coconut shrimp

dipping sauce

- ½ **cup orange marmalade**
- ⅓ **cup Thai chili sauce**
- 1 **teaspoon prepared horseradish**
- ½ **teaspoon salt**

shrimp

- 1 **cup flat beer**
- 1 **cup all-purpose flour**
- 2 **cups sweetened flaked coconut, divided**
- 2 **tablespoons sugar**
- 16 **to 20 large raw shrimp, peeled and deveined (with tails on), patted dry**

1 For dipping sauce, combine marmalade, chili sauce, horseradish and salt in small bowl; mix well. Cover and refrigerate until ready to serve.

2 For shrimp, whisk beer, flour, ½ cup coconut and sugar in large bowl until well blended. Place remaining 1½ cups coconut in medium bowl.

3 Preheat air fryer to 390°F. Line basket with parchment paper; spray with nonstick cooking spray.

4 Dip shrimp in beer batter, then in coconut, turning to coat completely. Cook in batches 6 to 8 minutes, turning halfway through cooking, until golden brown. Serve with dipping sauce.

Makes 4 servings

lemon-pepper chicken

⅓ cup lemon juice

¼ cup finely chopped onion

2 tablespoons olive oil

1 tablespoon packed brown sugar

1 tablespoon black pepper

3 cloves garlic, minced

2 teaspoons grated lemon peel

½ teaspoon salt

4 boneless skinless chicken breasts (about 1 pound)

1 Combine lemon juice, onion, oil, brown sugar, pepper, garlic, lemon peel and salt in small bowl; stir to blend. Pour marinade over chicken in large resealable food storage bag. Seal bag; knead to coat. Refrigerate at least 4 hours or overnight.

2 Preheat air fryer to 370°F. Line basket with parchment paper or foil; spray with nonstick cooking spray.

3 Remove chicken from marinade; discard marinade. Cook in batches 15 to 20 minutes or until chicken is browned, cooked through (165°F) and no longer pink in center.

lemon-pepper chicken on mixed greens

Toss 4 cups spring greens; 1 cup grape tomatoes, halved; and ½ cup sliced red onion in large bowl. Top with Lemon-Pepper Chicken breast. Serve with herb viniagrette or your favorite salad dressing.

Makes 4 servings

peach bourbon bbq bacon-wrapped scallops

⅔ cup barbecue sauce

¼ cup peach preserves

1 tablespoon bourbon

16 to 20 slices bacon (do not use thick-cut)

16 to 20 medium sea scallops (about 1¼ pounds)

1 tablespoon olive oil

Salt and black pepper

Hot cooked herbed rice (optional)

1 Combine barbecue sauce, preserves and bourbon in small saucepan; bring to a simmer over medium heat. Reduce heat to low; simmer 10 minutes.

2 Preheat air fryer to 390°F. Cook bacon in batches 2 to 3 minutes; remove to paper towels to absorb excess oil. Cool slightly.

3 Working with 1 scallop at a time, wrap 1 slice bacon around each scallop; thread onto skewers.* Thread 4 or 5 bacon-wrapped scallops onto each skewer depending on size of scallops and length of skewers.

4 Preheat air fryer to 390°F.

5 Brush scallops lightly with oil; sprinkle with salt and pepper. Cook 8 to 10 minutes or until bacon is crispy and scallops are opaque, turning halfway through cooking and occasionally brushing with sauce. Serve scallops with remaining sauce over rice, if desired.

*If using wooden skewers, soak in water 30 minutes to prevent burning.

Makes 4 servings

steak, mushrooms & onions

¾ **pound boneless steak, cut into 1-inch cubes**

8 **ounces sliced mushrooms, cleaned and washed**

1 **small onion, chopped**

3 **tablespoons melted butter, divided**

1 **teaspoon Worcestershire sauce**

½ **teaspoon garlic powder**

½ **teaspoon salt**

¼ **teaspoon black pepper**

Hot cooked egg noodles (optional)

½ **teaspoon dried parsley flakes**

1 Combine steak pieces, mushrooms and onion in large bowl. Toss with 1½ tablespoons butter, Worcestershire sauce and garlic powder.

2 Preheat air fryer to 390°F. Line basket with foil. Cook steak mixture 10 to 12 minutes, shaking occasionally, until steak is cooked.

3 Remove steak mixture to large bowl. Toss with remaining 1½ tablespoons butter, salt and pepper.

4 Serve over noodles, if desired. Sprinkle with parsley flakes.

Makes 4 servings

turkey breast with roasted squash

4 cups water

¼ cup coarse salt

⅓ cup packed brown sugar

1 frozen turkey breast roast
    (3 pounds), thawed

3 tablespoons melted butter

Salt and black pepper

2 medium zucchini *or*
    1 medium zucchini and
    1 medium yellow squash,
    cut into slices

1 tablespoon olive oil

1 Combine water, coarse salt and brown sugar in medium saucepan. Bring to a boil. Remove from heat; stir and let cool about 20 to 30 minutes or until room temperature.

2 Remove packaging from turkey breast, leaving netting in place. Place in large resealable food storage bag. Pour liquid over turkey; seal and place in large bowl. Refrigerate 6 hours or overnight.

3 Preheat air fryer to 390°F. Remove turkey from liquid, discarding liquid. Dry turkey with paper towels. Brush with half of butter.

4 Cook turkey, with netting in place, 15 minutes, turning halfway through cooking. Remove netting. *Reduce temperature to 350°F.* Brush turkey with remaining butter; cook 15 minutes. Turn, cook 12 to 15 minutes or until turkey reaches internal temperature of 165°F. Remove turkey; let stand 10 minutes.

5 Slice turkey. Season with salt and pepper.

6 Meanwhile, toss zucchini with oil in medium bowl. Preheat air fryer to 370°F. Cook 10 to 12 minutes or until tender and browned. Serve with turkey.

Makes 8 servings

lemon-pepper shrimp on garlic spinach

2½ teaspoons olive oil, divided

3 tablespoons lemon juice, divided

½ teaspoon ground black pepper

¼ teaspoon paprika

¼ teaspoon garlic powder

1 pound uncooked medium shrimp, peeled and deveined (with tails on)

2 cloves garlic, minced

8 ounces fresh baby spinach leaves (about 8 cups lightly packed), washed

¼ cup water

Lemon wedges (optional)

1 Combine 1½ teaspoons oil, 1 tablespoon lemon juice, pepper, paprika and garlic powder in medium bowl. Add shrimp; toss to coat.

2 Preheat air fryer to 390°F. Spray basket with nonstick cooking spray.

3 Cook 6 to 8 minutes or until shrimp are firm and no longer pink.

4 Meanwhile, heat remaining 1 teaspoon oil in small skillet over medium-high heat. Add garlic; cook 1 minute. Add spinach and water. Cook 4 to 5 minutes or until spinach is wilted. Drain; keep warm.

5 Serve shrimp over spinach. Serve with lemon wedges.

Makes 4 servings

eggplant parmesan

2 tablespoons olive oil

2 cloves garlic, minced

1 can (28 ounces) Italian whole tomatoes, undrained

½ cup water

1¼ teaspoons salt, divided

¼ teaspoon dried oregano

Pinch red pepper flakes

1 medium eggplant (about 1 pound)

⅓ cup all-purpose flour

Black pepper

⅔ cup milk

1 egg

1 cup Italian-seasoned dry bread crumbs

1 cup (4 ounces) shredded mozzarella cheese

Chopped fresh parsley (optional)

1. Heat oil in medium saucepan over medium heat. Add garlic; cook and stir 2 minutes or until softened (do not brown). Crush tomatoes with hands (in bowl or in can); add to saucepan with juices from can. Stir in water, 1 teaspoon salt, oregano and red pepper flakes; bring to a simmer. Reduce heat to medium-low; cook 45 minutes, stirring occasionally.

2. Meanwhile, prepare eggplant. Cut eggplant crosswise into ¼-inch slices. Combine flour, remaining ¼ teaspoon salt and black pepper in shallow dish. Beat milk and egg in another shallow dish. Place bread crumbs in third shallow dish.

3. Coat both sides of eggplant slices with flour mixture, shaking off excess. Dip in egg mixture, letting excess drip back into dish. Roll in bread crumbs to coat.

4. Preheat air fryer to 370°F. Spray basket with nonstick cooking spray. Cook in batches 10 to 12 minutes or until golden brown. Remove to plate; cover loosely with foil to keep warm.

5. Spray 9×9-inch* baking dish with cooking spray. Arrange eggplant slices overlapping in baking dish; top with half of warm marinara sauce. (Reserve remaining marinara sauce for pasta or another use.) Sprinkle with cheese.

6. Cook 1 to 2 minutes or just until cheese is melted and beginning to brown. Garnish with parsley.

If your air fryer is on the smaller side, you may need to use 2 smaller baking dishes.

Makes 4 servings

bourbon-marinated salmon

¼ **cup packed brown sugar**

¼ **cup bourbon**

¼ **cup soy sauce**

2 **tablespoons lime juice**

1 **tablespoon grated fresh ginger**

1 **tablespoon minced garlic**

¼ **teaspoon black pepper**

4 **salmon fillets (4 ounces each)**

2 **tablespoons minced green onion**

1 Combine brown sugar, bourbon, soy sauce, lime juice, ginger, garlic and pepper in medium bowl; mix well. Reserve ¼ cup mixture for serving; set aside.

2 Place salmon in large resealable food storage bag. Pour remaining marinade over salmon; seal bag and turn to coat. Marinate in refrigerator 2 to 4 hours, turning occasionally.

3 Preheat air fryer to 390°F. Remove salmon from marinade; discard marinade.

4 Cook salmon 8 to 10 minutes or until fish begins to flake when tested with fork. Brush with reserved marinade mixture; sprinkle with green onion.

Makes 4 servings

island fish tacos

coleslaw

- 1 medium jicama (about 12 ounces), peeled and shredded
- 2 cups packaged coleslaw mix
- 3 tablespoons finely chopped fresh cilantro
- ¼ cup lime juice
- ¼ cup vegetable oil
- 3 tablespoons white vinegar
- 2 tablespoons mayonnaise
- 1 tablespoon honey
- 1 teaspoon salt

salsa

- 2 medium fresh tomatoes, diced (about 2 cups)
- ½ cup finely chopped red onion
- ¼ cup finely chopped fresh cilantro
- 2 tablespoons lime juice
- 2 tablespoons minced jalapeño pepper
- 1 teaspoon salt

tacos

- 1 to 1¼ pounds white fish such as tilapia or mahi mahi, cut into 3×1½-inch pieces
- Salt and black pepper
- 12 (6-inch) taco-size tortillas, heated
- Prepared guacamole (optional)

1 For coleslaw, combine jicama, coleslaw mix and 3 tablespoons cilantro in medium bowl. Whisk ¼ cup lime juice, ¼ cup oil, vinegar, mayonnaise, honey and 1 teaspoon salt in small bowl until well blended. Pour over vegetable mixture; stir to coat. Let stand at least 15 minutes for flavors to blend.

2 For salsa, place tomatoes in fine-mesh strainer; set in bowl or sink to drain 15 minutes. Remove to another medium bowl. Stir in onion, ¼ cup cilantro, 2 tablespoons lime juice, jalapeño pepper and 1 teaspoon salt; mix well.

3 For tacos, season both sides of fish with salt and black pepper. Preheat air fryer to 350°F. Spray basket with nonstick cooking spray. Cook fish in batches 8 to 10 minutes or until fish is opaque and begins to flake when tested with fork.

4 Break fish into bite-size pieces; serve in tortillas with coleslaw, salsa and guacamole, if desired.

Makes 4 servings

zesty italian chicken nuggets

- 2 **boneless skinless chicken breasts**
- ¼ **cup zesty Italian salad dressing**
- 2 **cloves garlic, minced**
- 1½ **teaspoons lime juice**
- 1 **tablespoon honey**
- ½ **teaspoon salt**
- ¼ **teaspoon black pepper**

1 Cut chicken into 1-inch chunks. Place in large resealable food storage bag.

2 Combine dressing, garlic, lime juice, honey, salt and pepper in medium bowl. Pour over chicken; marinate in refrigerator 30 minutes to 1 hour.

3 Preheat air fryer to 370°F. Line basket with parchment paper. Remove chicken from marinade; discard marinade. Cook 10 to 12 minutes or until chicken is no longer pink and cooked throughout (165°F).

Makes 4 servings

steak fajitas

¼ cup lime juice

¼ cup soy sauce

2 tablespoons vegetable oil

2 tablespoons honey

2 tablespoons Worcestershire sauce

2 cloves garlic, minced

½ teaspoon ground red pepper

1 pound flank steak, skirt steak or top sirloin

1 medium yellow onion, halved and cut into ¼-inch slices

1 green bell pepper, cut into ¼-inch strips

1 red bell pepper, cut into ¼-inch strips

Flour tortillas, warmed

Lime wedges (optional)

Optional toppings: pico de gallo, guacamole, sour cream, shredded lettuce and shredded Cheddar-Jack cheese

1 Combine lime juice, soy sauce, oil, honey, Worcestershire sauce, garlic and ground red pepper in medium bowl; mix well. Remove ¼ cup marinade to large bowl. Place steak in large resealable food storage bag. Pour remaining marinade over steak; seal bag and turn to coat. Marinate in refrigerator at least 2 hours or overnight. Add onion and bell peppers to bowl with ¼ cup marinade; toss to coat. Cover and refrigerate until ready to use.

2 Remove steak from marinade; discard marinade and pat steak dry with paper towels. Preheat air fryer to 390°F. Spray basket with nonstick cooking spray. Cook steak 10 to 12 minutes, shaking occasionally, until desired doneness.* Remove to large cutting board; tent with foil and let stand 10 minutes.

3 Add vegetable mixture** to air fryer; cook 8 to 10 minutes or until vegetables are crisp-tender and beginning to brown in spots, shaking occasionally.

4 Cut steak into thin slices across the grain. Serve with vegetables, tortillas, lime wedges and desired toppings.

*Temperature for medium rare should be 135°F, medium 145°F, medium well 150°F.

**If your air fryer is on the smaller side, you may need to cut steak in half and cook steak and vegetables in batches.

Makes 2 servings

garlic chicken with roasted vegetables

3 tablespoons olive oil, divided

1 teaspoon salt

1 teaspoon dried oregano

1 teaspoon paprika

½ teaspoon black pepper

2 cloves garlic, minced

4 boneless skinless chicken breasts (about 1 pound)

2 cups Brussels sprouts, trimmed and halved

2 small yellow onions, cut into wedges

1 cup frozen crinkle-cut carrots

Salt and black pepper (optional)

1 Combine 2 tablespoons oil, 1 teaspoon salt, oregano, paprika, ½ teaspoon pepper and garlic in small bowl. Brush over chicken.

2 Preheat air fryer to 370°F. Line basket with parchment paper. Cook chicken in batches 15 to 20 minutes or until chicken is browned and no longer pink in center (165°F). Remove from air fryer; keep warm.

3 Toss Brussels sprouts, onions and carrots with remaining 1 tablespoon oil in medium bowl; season with salt and pepper, if desired. *Increase air fryer temperature to 390°F.* Cook vegetables in batches 6 to 8 minutes or until tender and lightly browned.

Makes 4 servings

104

salmon and crab cakes

½ **pound cooked salmon**

½ **pound cooked crabmeat***

1 **egg, lightly beaten** *or*
 ¼ **cup cholesterol-free egg substitute**

1½ **tablespoons reduced-fat mayonnaise**

1 **tablespoon minced fresh parsley**

1 **teaspoon dried dill weed**

½ **teaspoon salt substitute**

½ **teaspoon black pepper**

½ **teaspoon mustard**

¼ **teaspoon reduced-sodium Worcestershire sauce**

¼ **cup plain dry bread crumbs**

Lump crabmeat works best.

1 Flake salmon and crabmeat into medium bowl. Add egg, mayonnaise, parsley, dill weed, salt substitute, pepper, mustard and Worcestershire sauce; stir until well blended.

2 Place bread crumbs in shallow dish. Drop heaping ⅓ cup salmon mixture into bread crumbs; shape into thick patty. Repeat with remaining mixture.

3 Preheat air fryer to 390°F. Spray basket with nonstick cooking spray. Cook 5 to 8 minutes, turning halfway through cooking, until golden brown.

Makes 4 servings

SIDES

cinnamon-honey glazed carrot chips

1 package (16 ounces) carrot chips or baby carrots

¼ cup honey

2 tablespoons butter

1 teaspoon ground cinnamon

½ teaspoon ground nutmeg

1 Preheat air fryer to 390°F. Line basket with parchment paper. Place carrots in medium bowl.

2 Combine honey and butter in small microwavable bowl; microwave on HIGH 30 seconds or until melted. Stir. Add cinnamon and nutmeg; stir.

3 Pour honey mixture over carrots; toss well.

4 Cook in single layer 12 to 15 minutes or until browned and slightly tender.

Makes 6 servings

garlic air-fried mushrooms >

1 pound mushrooms, cleaned and stems removed, halved

2 tablespoons olive oil

1 teaspoon garlic powder

1 teaspoon Italian seasoning

½ teaspoon salt

¼ teaspoon black pepper

Fresh chopped parsley (optional)

Lemon wedges (optional)

1 Preheat air fryer to 370°F.

2 Combine mushrooms, oil, garlic powder, Italian seasoning, salt and pepper in large bowl; toss well.

3 Cook 12 to 15 minutes, shaking occasionally during cooking, until tender and browned. Garnish as desired.

Makes 4 servings

savory stuffed tomatoes

2 large ripe tomatoes (1 to 1¼ pounds total)

¾ cup garlic- or Caesar-flavored croutons

¼ cup chopped pitted kalamata olives (optional)

2 tablespoons chopped fresh basil

1 clove garlic, minced

2 tablespoons grated Parmesan or Romano cheese

1 tablespoon olive oil

1 Cut tomatoes in half crosswise; discard seeds. Scrape out and reserve pulp. Set aside tomato shells.

2 Chop up tomato pulp; place in medium bowl. Add croutons, olives, if desired, basil and garlic; toss well. Spoon mixture into tomato shells. Sprinkle with Parmesan cheese; drizzle oil over shells.

3 Preheat air fryer to 350°F. Line basket with foil or parchment paper.

4 Cook 5 to 7 minutes or until heated through.

Makes 4 servings

stuffed air-fried avocado

1 avocado

⅓ cup seasoned panko bread crumbs

Salt and black pepper

5 cherry tomatoes, halved

¼ cup (1 ounce) shredded mozzarella cheese

1½ tablespoons grated Parmesan cheese

2 tablespoons fresh basil leaves, chopped

Balsamic glaze

1 Peel avocado. Slice in half, removing and discarding seed. Preheat air fryer to 370°F. Line basket with foil.

2 Place panko in shallow dish. Press avocado halves into panko, coating all sides well. Sprinkle with salt and pepper, as desired. Spray with nonstick olive oil cooking spray. Cook 6 to 8 minutes or until panko is lightly browned.

3 Combine tomatoes, mozzarella cheese and Parmesan cheese and basil in medium bowl, spoon into well of avocado. Cook 1 to 2 minutes or until cheese is lightly melted.

4 Drizzle with balsamic glaze before serving. Serve immediately.

Makes 2 servings

roasted green beans >

1 pound fresh green beans, cut into 2-inch pieces

1 yellow onion, thinly sliced

½ pound sliced mushrooms

1 teaspoon minced garlic

½ teaspoon salt

¼ teaspoon black pepper

1 tablespoon oil

1 Preheat air fryer to 370°F. Spray basket with nonstick cooking spray.

2 Combine green beans, onion, mushrooms, garlic, salt and pepper in large bowl. Add oil; toss well to coat.

3 Cook 14 to 16 minutes, shaking halfway through cooking, until vegetables are tender and browned.

Makes 4 to 6 servings

olive twists

1 package (8 ounces) refrigerated crescent roll dough

1 egg white, beaten

12 pimiento-stuffed green olives, chopped

½ teaspoon paprika

1 Roll dough on lightly floured work surface to 12×8-inch rectangle. Cut crescent dough into 12 strips.

2 Brush dough lightly with egg white; sprinkle with olives and paprika. Wrap dough around olive filling.

3 Preheat air fryer to 370°F. Line basket with parchment paper.

4 Cook 5 to 7 minutes or until golden brown.

Makes 12 servings

simple golden corn bread

1¼ cups all-purpose flour

¾ cup yellow cornmeal

⅓ cup sugar

2 teaspoons baking powder

1 teaspoon salt

1¼ cups whole milk

¼ cup (½ stick) butter, melted

1 egg

Honey Butter (recipe follows, optional)

1 Preheat air fryer to 370°F. Spray 8-inch square baking dish or pan with nonstick cooking spray.

2 Combine flour, cornmeal, sugar, baking powder and salt in large bowl; mix well. Beat milk, butter and egg in medium bowl until well blended. Add to flour mixture; stir just until dry ingredients are moistened. Pour batter into prepared baking dish.

3 Cook 12 to 15 minutes or until golden brown and toothpick inserted into center comes out clean. Prepare Honey Butter, if desired. Serve with corn bread.

honey butter

Beat 6 tablespoons (¾ stick) softened butter and ¼ cup honey in medium bowl with electric mixer at medium-high speed until light and creamy.

Makes 9 to 12 servings

bang-bang cauliflower

1 head cauliflower
½ cup mayonnaise
¼ cup sweet chili sauce
1½ teaspoons hot pepper sauce
¼ teaspoon salt
⅛ teaspoon black pepper
¼ cup all-purpose flour
1 cup panko bread crumbs
2 green onions, chopped

1 Trim greens and stems from cauliflower. Cut into florets.

2 Combine mayonnaise, chili sauce, hot pepper sauce, salt and black pepper in small bowl. Remove half of mixture; set aside. Place flour and panko in separate shallow dishes.

3 Preheat air fryer to 390°F. Line basket with parchment paper.

4 Lightly coat cauliflower in flour. Dip in sauce mixture, coat with panko.

5 Cook in batches 8 to 10 minutes or until cauliflower is softened and browned.

6 Place cauliflower on serving plate; sprinkle with green onions. Serve with reserved sauce mixture.

Makes 4 to 6 servings

italian-style roasted vegetables

1 small eggplant, cut into chunks

1 small zucchini, cut into chunks

1 small red bell pepper, cut into chunks

1 small yellow bell pepper, cut into chunks

1 small onion, cut into chunks

10 cloves garlic

½ teaspoon salt

¼ teaspoon red pepper flakes

½ teaspoon dried basil

½ teaspoon dried oregano

1 tablespoon olive oil

1 teaspoon white vinegar

Shredded Parmesan cheese (optional)

1 Combine vegetables in large bowl. Toss with garlic, salt, red pepper flakes, basil, oregano, oil and vinegar.

2 Preheat air fryer to 390°F. Spray basket with nonstick cooking spray.

3 Cook in batches 12 to 15 minutes, shaking halfway during cooking, until vegetables are tender and browned.

4 Sprinkle with Parmesan cheese before serving, if desired.

Makes 6 servings

crispy brussels sprouts >

1 pound Brussels sprouts, halved

1½ tablespoons olive oil

2 tablespoons grated Parmesan cheese

¼ cup ground almonds

1 tablespoon everything bagel seasoning or seasoning of your choice

1 Preheat air fryer to 370°F.

2 Toss Brussels sprouts, oil, Parmesan cheese, almonds and bagel seasoning in large bowl.

3 Cook 8 to 10 minutes, shaking occasionally during cooking, until Brussels sprouts are browned and crispy.

Makes 4 servings

air-fried cauliflower florets

1 head cauliflower

1 tablespoon olive oil

3 tablespoons grated Parmesan cheese

2 tablespoons panko bread crumbs

½ teaspoon salt

½ teaspoon chopped fresh parsley

¼ teaspoon ground black pepper

1 Cut cauliflower into florets. Place in large bowl. Drizzle with oil. Sprinkle Parmesan cheese, panko, salt, parsley and pepper over cauliflower; toss to coat.

2 Preheat air fryer to 390°F. Spray basket with nonstick cooking spray.

3 Cook in batches 12 to 15 minutes, shaking every 5 minutes during cooking, until browned.

Makes 4 servings

garlic air-fried fries >

2 large potatoes, peeled and cut into matchstick strips

2 teaspoons plus 1 tablespoon olive oil, divided

1½ teaspoons minced garlic

½ teaspoon dried parsley flakes

½ teaspoon salt

¼ teaspoon ground black pepper

Ketchup, blue cheese or ranch dressing (optional)

1 Combine potato strips and 2 teaspoons oil in medium bowl; toss well.

2 Preheat air fryer to 390°F. Line basket with parchment paper.

3 Cook potatoes in batches 8 to 10 minutes, tossing occasionally, until golden brown and crispy.

4 While fries are cooking, combine remaining 1 tablespoon oil, garlic, parsley flakes, salt and pepper in small bowl.

5 Toss warm fries with garlic sauce. Serve immediately with ketchup, blue cheese or ranch dressing, if desired.

Makes 4 servings

air-fried corn-on-the-cob

2 teaspoons butter, melted

¼ teaspoon salt

½ teaspoon black pepper

½ teaspoon chopped fresh parsley

2 ears corn, husks and silks removed

Foil

Grated Parmesan cheese (optional)

1 Combine butter, salt, pepper and parsley in small bowl. Brush corn with butter mixture. Wrap each ear of corn in foil.*

2 Preheat air fryer to 390°F. Cook 6 to 8 minutes, turning halfway through cooking. Sprinkle with Parmesan cheese before serving, if desired.

If your air fryer basket is on the smaller side, you may need to break ears of corn in half to fit.

Makes 2 servings

garlic knots

4 tablespoons (½ stick) butter, divided

1 tablespoon olive oil

1 tablespoon minced garlic

½ teaspoon salt

¼ teaspoon garlic powder

1 package (about 11 ounces) refrigerated bread dough

½ cup grated Parmesan cheese

2 tablespoons chopped fresh parsley

½ teaspoon dried oregano

1 Melt 2 tablespoons butter in small saucepan over low heat. Add oil, garlic, salt and garlic powder; cook over very low heat 5 minutes. Pour into small bowl; set aside.

2 Roll out dough into 8×10-inch rectangle. Cut into 20 squares. Roll each piece into 8-inch rope; tie in a knot. Brush knots with garlic mixture.

3 Preheat air fryer to 370°F. Line basket with parchment paper.

4 Cook in batches 8 to 10 minutes or until knots are lightly browned. Meanwhile, melt remaining 2 tablespoons butter. Combine Parmesan cheese, parsley and oregano in small bowl; mix well. Brush melted butter over warm knots; immediately sprinkle with cheese mixture. Cool slightly; serve warm.

Makes 20 knots

potato balls

2 cups refrigerated leftover mashed potatoes*

2 tablespoons all-purpose flour, plus additional for rolling balls

⅔ cup shredded Cheddar cheese

¼ cup chopped green onions

1 large egg

½ teaspoon salt

¼ teaspoon black pepper

1½ cups seasoned dry bread crumbs

If you don't have leftover potatoes, prepare 2 cups instant mashed potatoes and refrigerate at least 1 hour.

1 Combine potatoes, 2 tablespoons flour, cheese and green onions in large bowl. Scoop out about 2 tablespoons mixture and roll into a 1-inch ball, adding additional flour, if necessary, making about 20 balls.

2 Beat egg, salt and pepper in medium bowl. Place bread crumbs in shallow dish. Dip balls in egg, letting excess drip back into bowl, then roll in bread crumbs until fully coated. Place on baking sheet; refrigerate 30 minutes.

3 Preheat air fryer to 390°F. Spray basket with nonstick cooking spray.

4 Cook in batches 8 to 10 minutes or until balls are browned and heated through.

Makes 20 balls

zucchini tomato rounds

2 large zucchini

Foil

½ cup cherry tomatoes, sliced

1 tablespoon olive oil

2 cloves garlic, minced

2 teaspoons Italian seasoning

1 teaspoon grated Parmesan cheese

1 Cut zucchini into thin slices three-fourths of the way down (do not cut all the way through). Place zucchini on foil sprayed with nonstick cooking spray.

2 Place tomato slices between each zucchini slice. Combine oil and garlic in small bowl. Drizzle over zucchini. Sprinkle with Italian seasoning and Parmesan cheese. Wrap foil around zucchini.

3 Preheat air fryer to 390°F. Place foil packets in basket. Cook 10 to 12 minutes or until browned and softened.

Makes 4 servings

curly air-fried fries

2 large russet potatoes, unpeeled

¼ cup thinly sliced onion

1 teaspoon vegetable oil

½ teaspoon salt

¼ teaspoon black pepper

Honey mustard dipping sauce, ketchup or other favorite dipping sauce

1 Spiral potatoes with thick spiral blade of spiralizer.*

2 Place potatoes and onion in large bowl; drizzle with oil. Toss well.

3 Preheat air fryer to 390°F. Line basket with parchment paper. Cook 10 to 12 minutes or until golden brown and crispy, shaking occasionally during cooking. Sprinkle with salt and pepper.

4 Serve with dipping sauce.

If you do not have a spiralizer, cut potatoes into thin strips.

Makes 4 servings

garlic roasted olives and tomatoes >

1 cup assorted olives, pitted

1 cup grape tomatoes, halved

4 cloves garlic, sliced

1 tablespoon olive oil

1 tablespoon herbes de Provence

1 Pat olives dry with paper towels.

2 Combine olives, tomatoes, garlic and oil in small bowl. Toss with herbes de Provence; mix well.

3 Preheat air fryer to 370°F. Cook 5 to 7 minutes or until browned and blistered, shaking occasionally during cooking. Remove to bowl.

serving suggestion

Toss with hot cooked pasta for a main dish.

Makes about 2 cups

cheesy garlic bread

1 loaf (about 8 ounces) Italian bread

¼ cup (½ stick) butter, softened

4 cloves garlic, diced

2 tablespoons grated Parmesan cheese

1 cup (4 ounces) shredded mozzarella cheese

1 Cut bread in half horizontally. Spread cut sides of bread evenly with butter; top with garlic. Sprinkle with Parmesan and mozzarella cheeses.

2 Preheat air fryer to 370°F. Line basket with foil.

3 Cook 5 to 6 minutes or until cheese is melted and golden brown. Cut crosswise into slices. Serve warm.

Makes 4 to 6 servings

roasted potatoes and onions with herbs

2 pounds unpeeled red potatoes, cut into 1½-inch pieces

1 sweet onion, such as Vidalia or Walla Walla, coarsely chopped

2 tablespoons olive oil

2 cloves garlic, minced

½ teaspoon salt

¼ teaspoon black pepper

¼ cup packed chopped mixed fresh herbs, such as basil, chives, parsley, oregano, rosemary leaves, sage, tarragon and thyme

1 Place potatoes and onion in large bowl. Combine oil, garlic, salt and pepper in small bowl. Drizzle over potatoes and onion; toss well to coat.

2 Preheat air fryer to 390°F. Line basket with foil.

3 Cook 18 to 20 minutes, shaking occasionally during cooking, until potatoes are tender and browned. Remove to large bowl. Add herbs; toss well.

Makes 6 servings

pepperoni bread

1 package (about 14 ounces) refrigerated pizza dough

8 slices provolone cheese

20 to 30 slices pepperoni (about ½ of 6-ounce package)

¾ cup (3 ounces) shredded mozzarella cheese

½ cup grated Parmesan cheese

½ teaspoon Italian seasoning

1 egg, beaten

Marinara sauce, heated

1 Unroll pizza dough on lightly floured surface; cut dough in half.

2 Working with one half at a time, arrange half the provolone slices on half the dough. Top with half the pepperoni, half the mozzarella and Parmesan cheese and half the Italian seasoning. Repeat with other half dough and toppings.

3 Fold top half of dough over filling; press edges with fork or pinch edges to seal.

4 Preheat air fryer to 390°F. Line basket with parchment paper. Transfer one bread to basket. Brush with egg.

5 Cook 8 to 10 minutes or until crust is golden brown. Remove to wire rack to cool slightly. Repeat with other bread. Cut crosswise into slices; serve warm with marinara sauce.

Makes about 6 servings

KIDS' FAVORITES

chocolate monkey sandwiches

2 slices thick white bread or 1 flatbread

1 tablespoon butter, softened

1 tablespoon chocolate hazelnut spread

1 tablespoon peanut butter

1 small banana, cut into thin slices

1. Spread one side of each bread slice with butter. (If using flatbread, spread butter on one side.)

2. Place bread butter-side down on work surface. Spread one slice bread with hazelnut spread. Spread other slice bread with peanut butter. (If using flatbread, spread on each half.)

3. Top chocolate side with banana slices. Top banana slices with peanut butter-covered bread. Cut sandwich in half.

4. Preheat air fryer to 370°F. Cook sandwich halves 5 to 7 minutes or until bread is lightly browned.

Makes 2 servings

air-fried salmon nuggets with broccoli

1 **pound skinless salmon fillet**

2 **eggs**

1 **cup plain dry bread crumbs**

¾ **teaspoon salt, divided**

2 **cups broccoli florets**

1 **tablespoon olive oil**

Sweet and sour sauce or other favorite dipping sauce (optional)

1 Cut salmon into 1-inch chunks.

2 Whisk eggs in small bowl. Combine bread crumbs and ½ teaspoon salt in shallow dish. Dip salmon chunks in eggs, letting excess drip back into bowl. Coat evenly with bread crumbs. Set on plate; spray lightly with nonstick cooking spray.

3 Preheat air fryer to 390°F. Spray basket with cooking spray.

4 Cook in batches 3 to 4 minutes; flip nuggets over. Spray with cooking spray. Cook 3 to 4 minutes or until golden brown. Remove to plate; keep warm.

5 Meanwhile, toss broccoli with oil in large bowl. Sprinkle with remaining ¼ teaspoon salt. Cook 6 to 8 minutes or until browned and crispy.

6 Serve nuggets and broccoli with sweet and sour sauce, if desired.

substitute

Try garlic-herb or Italian-seasoned bread crumbs instead of plain.

Makes 5 servings

tasty turkey turnovers

1 package (about 8 ounces) refrigerated crescent roll sheet

2 tablespoons honey mustard, plus additional for serving

3 ounces thinly sliced lean deli turkey breast

¾ cup packaged broccoli coleslaw mix

1 egg white, beaten

1 Roll out dough onto lightly floured surface. Using a wide glass or cookie cutter, cut into 3½-inch circles. Spread 2 tablespoons honey mustard lightly over dough circles; top with turkey and coleslaw mix. Brush edges of dough with egg white. Fold circles in half; press edges with tines of fork to seal. Brush with egg white.

2 Preheat air fryer to 370°F. Spray basket with nonstick cooking spray.

3 Cook in batches 6 to 7 minutes or until golden brown. Let stand 5 minutes before serving. Serve warm or at room temperature with additional honey mustard for dipping, if desired.

Makes 6 servings

shortbread cookie sticks

- 1¼ cups all-purpose flour
- 3 tablespoons sugar
- ½ cup (1 stick) butter
- ½ cup chocolate chips
- 1 tablespoon whipping cream
- ¼ cup sprinkles

1 Combine flour and sugar in large bowl; cut in butter with pastry cutter until fine crumbs form. Using damp hands, form dough into a ball and knead until smooth.

2 Roll dough to ½-inch thickness on lightly floured work surface. Cut into ½-inch×4-inch sticks.

3 Preheat air fryer to 350°F.

4 Cook sticks in batches 5 to 7 minutes or until lightly browned. Remove from basket; cool completely.

5 Combine chocolate chips and cream in small microwavable bowl. Cover and microwave 30 seconds or until melted; stir. Dip sticks in chocolate. Top with sprinkles. Place on plate or cookie sheet. Refrigerate until chocolate is set.

Makes 1½ dozen cookies

air-fried pepperoni pizza bagels

4 Homemade Air-Fried Bagels (recipe follows) or store-bought bagels

¼ cup marinara sauce

¼ cup mini pepperoni slices

¼ cup (1 ounce) shredded mozzarella cheese

Dried oregano

1 Cut bagels in half lengthwise. Top each half with equal amount sauce, pepperoni and cheese.

2 Preheat air fryer to 350°F. Line basket with foil or parchment paper. Cook 3 to 5 minutes or until cheese is melted and browned. Sprinkle with oregano.

Makes 4 servings

homemade air-fried bagels

1 cup self-rising flour

1 cup plain nonfat Greek yogurt

1 large egg, beaten

Sesame seeds, poppy seeds, dried onion flakes, everything bagel seasoning (optional)

1 Combine flour and yogurt in bowl of electric stand mixer with dough hook.* Beat 2 to 3 minutes or until mixture is well combined. Place dough on lightly floured surface; knead by hand about 4 to 5 minutes or until dough is smooth and elastic. Form dough into a ball.

2 Cut into 4 equal portions. Roll each into a ball. Pull and stretch dough to create desired shape, inserting finger into center to create hole. Repeat with remaining dough.

3 Preheat air fryer to 330°F. Line basket with parchment paper. Place bagels on parchment; brush with egg. Sprinkle with desired toppings. Cook 8 to 10 minutes or until lightly browned.

*Or, use heavy spatula in large bowl to combine mixture.

Makes 4 servings

chicken corndog bites

1 package (8 ounces)
   refrigerated dough
   sheet

1 package (9 ounces)
   Italian-seasoned cooked
   chicken breast strips

   Mustard

   Ketchup

1 Unroll dough on lightly floured surface. Roll into 12×9-inch rectangle; cut into 16 (4×3-inch) pieces.

2 Cut chicken strips in half crosswise. Place one piece of chicken on each piece of dough; wrap dough around chicken and seal, pressing edges together tightly.

3 Preheat air fryer to 370°F. Line basket with parchment paper or foil.

4 Cook in batches 5 to 7 minutes or until light golden brown. Decorate with mustard and ketchup. Serve warm with additional mustard and ketchup for dipping.

Makes 16 bites

foxy face foldovers

1 ripe medium banana

1 package (17¼ ounces) frozen puff pastry sheets (2 sheets), thawed according to package directions

9 tablespoons semisweet chocolate chips, divided

36 sliced almonds

18 dried sweetened cranberries

1 Peel banana and place in small resealable food storage bag; seal. Squeeze banana into a pulp.

2 Place puff pastry sheets on lightly floured surface. Cut each sheet into 9 even squares.

3 Place 1 teaspoon chocolate chips in center of each square. Cut small corner off one end of banana-filled bag. Squeeze about ½ teaspoon banana pulp over chocolate chips.

4 Fold each puff pastry square into a triangle by bringing opposing corners together; press edges together with tines of fork to seal.

5 Preheat air fryer to 370°F. Cook in batches 8 to 10 minutes or until crispy and golden brown. Remove to wire racks to cool completely.

6 When pastries are cool, place remaining 6 tablespoons chocolate chips in small resealable food storage bag. Microwave on HIGH 30 seconds or until melted. Cut small corner off one end of bag; use melted chocolate to create ears and whiskers and to attach almonds and cranberries for eyes and noses.

Makes 18 pastries

veggie pizza pitas

1 whole wheat pita bread round, cut in half horizontally (to make 2 rounds)

2 tablespoons pizza sauce

½ teaspoon dried basil

⅛ teaspoon red pepper flakes (optional)

½ cup sliced mushrooms

¼ cup thinly sliced green bell pepper

¼ cup thinly sliced red onion

½ cup (2 ounces) shredded mozzarella cheese

1 teaspoon grated Parmesan cheese

1 Arrange pita rounds, rough sides up, in single layer on parchment paper. Spread 1 tablespoon pizza sauce evenly over each round to within ¼ inch of edge. Sprinkle with basil and red pepper flakes, if desired. Top with mushrooms, bell pepper and onion. Sprinkle with mozzarella cheese.

2 Preheat air fryer to 370°F.

3 Cook in batches 5 to 7 minutes or until cheese melts. Sprinkle ½ teaspoon Parmesan cheese over each pita round.

note

These pitas can be served as appetizers, as well.

Makes 2 servings

piggies in a basket >

1 package (8 ounces) refrigerated crescent roll dough

1 package (about 12 ounces) cocktail franks

1 Cut crescent dough into strips. Wrap dough around each frank.

2 Preheat air fryer to 350°F.

3 Cook in batches 3 to 4 minutes or until golden brown.

Makes 4 servings

tuna pies

1 package (8 ounces) refrigerated crescent dough sheet

1 can (about 5 ounces) water-packed tuna, drained

1 tablespoon mayonnaise

1 cup (4 ounces) shredded Cheddar cheese

1 Preheat air fryer to 370°F. Spray 4 ramekins with nonstick cooking spray.

2 Roll out dough onto lightly floured surface to 12×8-inch rectangle. Cut into 4 (6×4-inch) rectangles. Press dough into bottoms and up sides of prepared ramekins.

3 Combine tuna and mayonnaise in small bowl; mix gently. Spoon tuna mixture evenly over dough; sprinkle with cheese.

4 Cook in batches 8 to 10 minutes or until dough is golden brown. Let cool slightly before serving.

variation

You can add vegetables, like broccoli, celery or peas, to this recipe, as well as trying other types of cheese, like mozzarella or Swiss.

Makes 4 servings

crispy ranch chicken bites

1 **pound boneless skinless chicken breasts**

½ **cup ranch salad dressing, plus additional for serving**

2 **cups panko bread crumbs**

1 Cut chicken into 1-inch cubes. Place ½ cup dressing in small bowl. Spread panko in shallow dish. Dip chicken in dressing; shake off excess. Roll in panko to coat. Spray chicken with nonstick cooking spray.

2 Preheat air fryer to 370°F. Line basket with parchment paper.

3 Cook in batches 8 to 10 minutes or until golden brown and cooked through. Serve with additional ranch dressing.

serving suggestion

Serve with fresh vegetable sticks like celery, carrot and bell peppers.

Makes 6 servings

SNACKS

toasted tortellini

2 eggs

2 tablespoons milk

⅔ cup Italian-seasoned dry bread crumbs

1 teaspoon garlic powder

2 tablespoons grated Parmesan cheese

½ teaspoon salt

1 package (9 ounces) refrigerated tortellini

Fresh parsley, chopped

Marinara sauce, warmed

1 Whisk eggs and milk in medium bowl. Combine bread crumbs, garlic powder, Parmesan cheese and salt in shallow dish.

2 Preheat air fryer to 370°F. Spray basket with nonstick cooking spray.

3 Dip tortellini in egg mixture, letting excess drip back into bowl. Roll tortellini in bread crumb mixture. Spray tortellini with cooking spray.

4 Cook in single layer 6 to 8 minutes or until crispy and golden brown.

5 Sprinkle with parsley. Serve with warmed marinara sauce.

Makes 6 to 8 servings

guacamole with corn tortilla chips

2 large ripe avocados

2 teaspoons fresh lime juice

¼ cup finely chopped red onion

2 tablespoons chopped fresh cilantro

½ jalapeño pepper, finely chopped

½ teaspoon salt

1 Cut avocados in half lengthwise around pits. Remove pits. Scoop avocados into large bowl; sprinkle with lime juice and toss to coat. Mash to desired consistency with fork or potato masher.

2 Add onion, cilantro, jalapeño pepper and ½ teaspoon salt; stir gently until well blended. Taste and add additional salt, if desired.

Makes 2 cups

corn tortilla chips

6 (6-inch) corn tortillas, preferably day-old

½ teaspoon salt

Guacamole (optional)

1 If tortillas are fresh, let stand, uncovered, in single layer on wire rack 1 to 2 hours to dry slightly.

2 Stack tortillas; cut tortillas into 6 equal wedges. Spray tortillas generously with nonstick olive oil cooking spray.

3 Preheat air fryer to 370°F.

4 Cook in batches 5 to 6 minutes, shaking halfway through cooking. Sprinkle with salt. Serve with guacamole.

note

Tortilla chips are best eaten fresh, but can be stored, tightly covered, in a cool place 2 or 3 days.

Makes 3 dozen chips (about 12 servings)

everything seasoning dip with bagel chips

2 large bagels, sliced vertically into rounds

1 container (12 ounces) whipped cream cheese

1½ tablespoons green onion, finely chopped (green part only)

1 teaspoon dried minced onion

1 teaspoon granulated garlic

1 teaspoon sesame seeds

1 teaspoon poppy seeds

¼ teaspoon kosher salt

1 Preheat air fryer to 350°F.

2 Coat bagel rounds generously with butter-flavored nonstick cooking spray. Cook 7 to 8 minutes, shaking occasionally, until golden brown.

3 Meanwhile, combine cream cheese, green onion, minced onion, garlic, sesame seeds, poppy seeds and salt in medium bowl until well blended.

4 Serve chips with dip.

Makes 2 cups dip (about 16 servings)

air-fried bowtie bites

½ **pound uncooked bowtie (farfalle) pasta or your favorite shaped pasta (shells, tubes)**

1½ **tablespoons olive oil**

¼ **cup grated Parmesan cheese**

½ **teaspoon salt**

½ **teaspoon garlic powder**

¼ **teaspoon black pepper**

Marinara sauce, warmed (optional)

1 Prepare pasta according to package directions, until al dente. Drain but do not rinse. Transfer pasta to large bowl.

2 Preheat air fryer to 390°F.

3 Drizzle pasta with oil; toss with Parmesan cheese, salt, garlic powder and pepper.

4 Cook pasta in single layer* 10 to 12 minutes, shaking occasionally until lightly browned and crisp around the edges. Season with additional salt and pepper, if desired.

5 Serve with marinara sauce for dipping, if desired.

Cook in batches, if necessary.

Makes 8 to 10 servings

roasted chickpeas

1 can (about 15 ounces) chickpeas, rinsed and drained

1 tablespoon olive oil

¼ teaspoon salt

¼ teaspoon black pepper

¼ tablespoon chili powder

¼ teaspoon ground red pepper

1 lime, cut into wedges (optional)

1 Combine chickpeas, oil, salt and black pepper in large bowl; toss to mix well.

2 Preheat air fryer to 390°F.

3 Cook 8 to 10 minutes, shaking occasionally during cooking, until chickpeas begin to brown.

4 Sprinkle with chili powder and ground red pepper. Serve with lime wedges, if desired.

note

Great as a snack or as a topping for salads. Chickpeas offer a delicious crunch and healthier alternative to croutons.

Makes 1 cup (4 servings)

lavash chips with artichoke pesto

3 pieces lavash bread

¼ cup plus 2 tablespoons olive oil, divided

¾ teaspoon kosher salt, divided

1 can (14 ounces) artichoke hearts, rinsed and drained

½ cup chopped walnuts, toasted*

¼ cup packed fresh basil leaves

1 clove garlic, minced

2 tablespoons lemon juice

¼ cup grated Parmesan cheese

To toast nuts, cook in preheated 325°F parchment paper-lined air fryer 3 to 4 minutes or until golden brown.

1 Preheat air fryer to 370°F. Line basket with parchment paper.

2 Brush both sides of lavash with 2 tablespoons oil. Sprinkle with ¼ teaspoon salt. Cut to fit in air fryer, if necessary. Cook in batches 6 to 8 minutes, shaking occasionally, until lavash is crisp and browned. Cool on wire rack.

3 Place artichoke hearts, walnuts, basil, garlic, lemon juice and remaining ½ teaspoon salt in food processor; pulse about 12 times or until coarsely chopped. While food processor is running, slowly stream remaining ¼ cup oil until smooth. Add Parmesan cheese and pulse until blended.

4 Serve lavash with pesto.

note

You can also toast walnuts in preheated 350°F oven 6 to 8 minutes, if preferred.

Makes about 1½ cups pesto (8 servings)

kale chips

1 **large bunch kale (about 1 pound)**

1 **tablespoon olive oil**

1 **teaspoon garlic powder**

½ **teaspoon salt**

½ **teaspoon black pepper**

1 Wash kale and pat dry with paper towels. Remove center ribs and stems; discard. Cut leaves into 2- to 3-inch-wide pieces.

2 Combine kale leaves, oil, garlic powder, salt and pepper in large bowl; toss to coat.

3 Preheat air fryer to 390°F.

4 Cook in batches 3 to 4 minutes or until edges are lightly browned and leaves are crisp. Cool completely. Store in airtight container.

Makes 6 servings

SWEETS AND TREATS

toasted pound cake with berries and cream

1 package (10¾ ounces) frozen pound cake

2 tablespoons melted butter

1 cup fresh blackberries or blueberries

1 cup fresh raspberries or strawberries

Whipped topping, vanilla ice cream or prepared lemon curd

1 Cut pound cake into 8 slices. Brush both sides of cake with butter.

2 Preheat air fryer to 370°F. Cook in batches 5 to 7 minutes, turning halfway through cooking, until cake is lightly browned.

3 Serve with fresh berries, whipped topping, ice cream or lemon curd, as desired.

Makes 4 servings

fried pineapple with toasted coconut

1 **large pineapple, cored and cut into chunks**

½ **cup packed brown sugar**

1 **teaspoon ground cinnamon**

½ **teaspoon ground nutmeg**

½ **cup toasted coconut***

Ice cream or whipped cream (optional)

Chopped macadamia nuts (optional)

Maraschino cherries (optional)

*To toast coconut in air fryer, place coconut in small ramekin. Cook in preheated 350°F air fryer 2 to 3 minutes or until lightly browned.

1 Place pineapple chunks in large bowl. Combine brown sugar, cinnamon and nutmeg in small bowl; sprinkle over pineapple. Toss well. Refrigerate 30 minutes.

2 Preheat air fryer to 370°F. Spray basket with nonstick cooking spray.

3 Cook 6 to 8 minutes or until pineapple is browned and lightly crispy. Sprinkle with coconut. Serve with ice cream and/or macadamias, if desired. Garnish with maraschino cherry.

Makes 8 servings

hasselback apples

2 medium apples, unpeeled

Foil

2 tablespoons packed brown
   sugar

2 tablespoons finely
   chopped walnuts

½ teaspoon ground
   cinnamon

2 tablespoons butter, melted

½ cup vanilla ice cream
   (optional)

1 Cut apples in half vertically. Scoop out seeds. Lay flat side down; cut slits ⅛ inch apart almost all the way down. Place apples on foil; wrapping lightly up sides of apple.

2 Combine brown sugar, walnuts and cinnamon in small bowl. Brush butter over tops of apples, letting drip inside slits. Sprinkle apples with brown sugar mixture.

3 Preheat air fryer to 350°F. Place foil-wrapped apples in basket. Cook 12 to 15 minutes or until apples are softened and browned.

4 Serve with ice cream, if desired.

note

If apples brown too quickly on top, brush with additional melted butter.

Makes 4 servings

chocolate–peanut butter dessert wontons

24 wonton wrappers

½ cup peanut butter

½ cup chocolate hazelnut spread

Water

¼ cup chocolate sauce, warmed

2 tablespoons powdered sugar

1 Lay wontons on flat surface. Spoon about ½ teaspoon peanut butter and ½ teaspoon hazelnut spread in center of each wonton. Wet finger with water and spread around edges of wonton; fold into triangle using water to seal edges.

2 Preheat air fryer to 370°F. Cook wontons 4 to 5 minutes or until lightly browned.

3 Place wontons on serving plate. Drizzle with chocolate sauce and sprinkle with powdered sugar before serving.

Makes 2 dozen wontons

apple pie egg rolls

3 Granny Smith apples or other tart apples, peeled and chopped

½ cup packed brown sugar

1½ teaspoons ground cinnamon

1 teaspoon cornstarch

½ teaspoon vanilla

8 egg roll wrappers

2 tablespoons water

1 tablespoon melted butter

1 teaspoon cinnamon-sugar*

Caramel sauce, warmed (optional)

To make cinnamon-sugar, combine 1 teaspoon sugar with ¼ teaspoon ground cinnamon.

1 Combine apples, brown sugar, 1½ teaspoons cinnamon and cornstarch in medium saucepan. Heat over high heat 3 to 4 minutes, stirring occasionally. Turn heat to low; cover. Cook 5 to 6 minutes or until apples are tender. Remove from heat; stir in vanilla.

2 Lay egg roll wrappers on dry surface. Brush water around edge of wrapper. Spoon about 1 to 2 tablespoons apple filling in center of wrapper; fold up sides and bottom of egg roll. Brush lightly with melted butter; sprinkle with cinnamon-sugar.

3 Preheat air fryer to 370°F. Spray basket with nonstick cooking spray.

4 Cook seam side down, in batches if necessary, 8 to 10 minutes or until lightly browned. Cool slightly. Serve with caramel sauce, if desired.

substitution

Try other fruits, like strawberries, raspberries or peaches, too!

Makes 8 servings

bloomin' baked apples

2 apples

2 tablespoons butter, melted

1 tablespoon packed brown
  sugar

1 tablespoon cinnamon-
  sugar*

  Vanilla ice cream
  (optional)

  Caramel sauce, warmed
  (optional)

*To make cinnamon-sugar,
combine 1 tablespoon sugar
with ½ teaspoon ground
cinnamon.*

1 Slice off top of apples, use a paring knife or apple
cutter to cut about 8 lengthwise slices through apple,
being careful not to cut all the way down to the
bottom. Remove and discard seeds and core.

2 Combine butter, brown sugar and cinnamon-sugar in
small bowl. Place apples in small dish or ramekin. Brush
butter mixture over apples, letting it drip down the
cuts.

3 Preheat air fryer to 370°F. Cook apples 15 to 20 minutes
or until apples are softened and light brown.

4 Serve with ice cream and drizzle with caramel sauce,
as desired.

Makes 2 servings

apple pie pockets

2 pieces lavash bread, each cut into 4 rectangles

2 tablespoons melted butter

¾ cup apple pie filling

1 egg, lightly beaten with 1 teaspoon water

½ cup powdered sugar

⅛ teaspoon ground cinnamon

2½ teaspoons milk

1 Brush one side of each piece of lavash with butter. Place half of the pieces, buttered-side down, on work surface. Spoon 3 tablespoons pie filling in center of each lavash, leaving ½-inch border uncovered. Using pastry brush, brush border with egg wash. Top with remaining lavash pieces, buttered-side up. Using tines of fork, press edges together to seal. Use paring knife to cut 3 small slits in center of each pie pocket.

2 Preheat air fryer to 370°F. Line basket with parchment paper.

3 Cook in batches 8 to 10 minutes or until crust is golden and crisp. Remove to wire rack; cool 15 minutes.

4 Combine powdered sugar, cinnamon and milk in small bowl; whisk until smooth. Drizzle over pockets; let stand 15 minutes to allow glaze to slightly set.

Makes 4 servings

chocolate fruit tarts

1 refrigerated pie crust (half of 15-ounce package)

1¼ cups prepared low-fat chocolate pudding (about 4 snack-size pudding cups)

Fresh sliced strawberries, raspberries, blackberries or favorite fruit

1 Spray 6 (2½-inch) silicone muffin cups with nonstick cooking spray. Unfold pie crust on lightly-floured surface. Let stand at room temperature 15 minutes.

2 Roll out pie crust on clean work surface; cut out 6 circles with 4-inch round cookie cutter. Place dough circles in muffin cups, pleating around sides of cups. (Press firmly to hold dough in place.) Prick bottom and sides with fork.

3 Preheat air fryer to 370°F. Cook in batches 8 to 10 minutes or until golden brown. Carefully remove tart shells from muffin cups. Cool completely on wire rack.

4 Fill each tart shell with about 3 tablespoons pudding; arrange fruit on top.

Makes 6 tarts

INDEX

A

Air-Fried Bowtie Bites, 166
Air-Fried Cauliflower Florets, 122
Air-Fried Corn-on-the-Cob, 124
Air-Fried Pepperoni Pizza Bagels, 148
Air-Fried Salmon Nuggets with Broccoli, 142

Appetizers
  Baked Salami, 30
  Buffalo-Style Oyster Mushrooms, 10
  Burger Bites, 18
  Caprese Portobellos, 24
  Crispy Mushrooms, 16
  Green Bean Fries, 8
  Loaded Tater Tots, 20
  Mini Pepper Nachos, 22
  Mozzarella Sticks, 7
  Parmesan Pickle Chips, 26
  Pepper Pizza Poppers, 14
  Sweet Cocktail Meatballs, 12
  Toasted Ravioli, 28
Apple Pie Egg Rolls, 182
Apple Pie Pockets, 186

Apples
  Apple Pie Egg Rolls, 182
  Apple Pie Pockets, 186
  Baked Apple Pancake, 40
  Bloomin' Baked Apples, 184
  Chicken Waldorf Salad, 54
  Hasselback Apples, 178

Avocados
  Guacamole with Corn Tortilla Chips, 162
  Stuffed Air-Fried Avocado, 112

B

Baked Apple Pancake, 40
Baked Salami, 30

Bananas
  Chocolate Monkey Sandwiches, 141
  Foxy Face Foldovers, 152
  Strawberry Banana French Toast, 36
Bang-Bang Cauliflower, 118

Beef
  Baked Salami, 30
  Beef Taquitos, 78
  Burger Bites, 18
  Classic Patty Melts, 66
  One-Bite Burgers, 74
  Steak Fajitas, 102
  Steak, Mushrooms & Onions, 88
  Sweet Cocktail Meatballs, 12
Beef Taquitos, 78
Biscuit Doughnuts, 46
Bloomin' Baked Apples, 184
Bourbon-Marinated Salmon, 96

Breads
  Biscuit Doughnuts, 46
  Cheesy Garlic Bread, 134
  Garlic Knots, 126
  Homemade Air-Fried Bagels, 148
  Olive Twists, 114
  Pepperoni Bread, 138
  Simple Golden Corn Bread, 116
  Strawberry Banana French Toast, 36

Breakfast
  Baked Apple Pancake, 40
  Biscuit Doughnuts, 46
  Breakfast Flats, 33
  Breakfast Pepperoni Flatbread, 42
  Broiled Grapefruit Your Way, 44
  Omelet Scramble, 38
  Ricotta Pancakes, 34
  Strawberry Banana French Toast, 36
Breakfast Flats, 33
Breakfast Pepperoni Flatbread, 42
Broiled Grapefruit Your Way, 44

Brussels Sprouts
  Crispy Brussels Sprouts, 122
  Garlic Chicken with Roasted Vegetables, 104
Buffalo-Style Oyster Mushrooms, 10
Burger Bites, 18
Buttermilk Air-Fried Chicken, 77

C

Caprese Portobellos, 24

Cauliflower
  Air-Fried Cauliflower Florets, 122
  Bang-Bang Cauliflower, 118
Cheesy Garlic Bread, 134

Chicken
  Buttermilk Air-Fried Chicken, 77
  Chicken Corndog Bites, 150
  Chicken Parmesan Sliders, 68
  Chicken Waldorf Salad, 54
  Crispy Ranch Chicken Bites, 158
  Garlic Chicken with Roasted Vegetables, 104
  Lemon-Pepper Chicken, 84
  Nashville-Style Hot Chicken Sandwich, 56
  Parmesan-Crusted Chicken, 80
  Strawberry Poppy Seed Chicken Salad, 64
  Zesty Italian Chicken Nuggets, 100
Chicken Corndog Bites, 150
Chicken Parmesan Sliders, 68
Chicken Waldorf Salad, 54

Chocolate
  Chocolate Fruit Tarts, 188
  Chocolate Monkey Sandwiches, 141
  Chocolate-Peanut Butter Dessert Wontons, 180
  Foxy Face Foldovers, 152
  Shortbread Cookie Sticks, 146
Chocolate Fruit Tarts, 188
Chocolate Monkey Sandwiches, 141
Chocolate-Peanut Butter Dessert Wontons, 180
Cinnamon-Honey Glazed Carrot Chips, 109
Classic Patty Melts, 66
Coconut Shrimp, 82

Corn
  Air-Fried Corn-on-the-Cob, 124
  Mini Pepper Nachos, 22
Crispy Brussels Sprouts, 122
Crispy Mushrooms, 16

Crispy Ranch Chicken Bites, 158
Curly Air-Fried Fries, 132

D

Dessert
  Apple Pie Egg Rolls, 182
  Apple Pie Pockets, 186
  Bloomin' Baked Apples, 184
  Chocolate Fruit Tarts, 188
  Chocolate-Peanut Butter
    Dessert Wontons, 180
  Fried Pineapple with Toasted
    Coconut, 176
  Hasselback Apples, 178
  Shortbread Cookie Sticks, 146
  Toasted Pound Cake with
    Berries and Cream, 175

E

Eggplant
  Eggplant Pizzas, 52
  Eggplant Parmesan, 94
  Italian-Style Roasted
    Vegetables, 120
Eggplant Pizzas, 52
Eggplant Parmesan, 94
Everything Seasoning Dip with
  Bagel Chips, 164

F

Fish & Seafood
  Air-Fried Salmon Nuggets with
    Broccoli, 142
  Bourbon-Marinated Salmon,
    96
  Coconut Shrimp, 82
  Island Fish Tacos, 98
  Lemon-Pepper Shrimp on
    Garlic Spinach, 92
  Peach Bourbon BBQ Bacon-
    Wrapped Scallops, 86
  Salmon and Crab Cakes, 106
  Salmon Croquettes, 49
  Shrimp and Spinach Salad, 58
  Tuna Pies, 156
Foxy Face Foldovers, 152
Fried Pineapple with Toasted
  Coconut, 176

G

Garlic Air-Fried Fries, 124
Garlic Air-Fried Mushrooms, 110
Garlic Chicken with Roasted
  Vegetables, 104
Garlic Knots, 126
Garlic Roasted Olives and
  Tomatoes, 134
Green Bean Fries, 8
Green Beans
  Green Bean Fries, 8
  Roasted Green Beans, 114
Guacamole with Corn Tortilla
  Chips, 162

H

Hasselback Apples, 178
Hawaiian Pizza Rolls, 72
Hearty Veggie Sandwich, 70
Homemade Air-Fried Bagels, 148

I

Island Fish Tacos, 98
Italian-Style Roasted Vegetables,
  120

K

Kale Chips, 172

L

Lavash Chips with Artichoke
  Pesto, 170
Lemon-Pepper Chicken, 84
Lemon-Pepper Shrimp on Garlic
  Spinach, 92
Loaded Tater Tots, 20

M

Mini Pepper Nachos, 22
Mozzarella Sticks, 7
Mushroom Po-Boys, 60
Mushrooms
  Buffalo-Style Oyster
    Mushrooms, 10
  Caprese Portobellos, 24
  Crispy Mushrooms, 16
  Garlic Air-Fried Mushrooms, 110
  Hearty Veggie Sandwich, 70

Mushroom Po-Boys, 60
Pizza Sandwich, 50
Steak, Mushrooms & Onions,
  88
Veggie Pizza Pitas, 154

N

Nashville-Style Hot Chicken
  Sandwich, 56

O

Olive Twists, 114
Omelet Scramble, 38
One-Bite Burgers, 74

P

Parmesan Pickle Chips, 26
Parmesan-Crusted Chicken, 80
Peach Bourbon BBQ Bacon-
  Wrapped Scallops, 86
Pepper Pizza Poppers, 14
Pepperoni Bread, 138
Piggies in a Basket, 156
Pineapple
  Fried Pineapple with Toasted
    Coconut, 176
  Hawaiian Pizza Rolls, 72
  Strawberry Poppy Seed
    Chicken Salad, 64
Pizza
  Air-Fried Pepperoni Pizza
    Bagels, 148
  Eggplant Pizzas, 52
  Hawaiian Pizza Rolls, 72
  Pepper Pizza Poppers, 14
  Pizza Sandwich, 50
  Veggie Pizza Pitas, 154
Pizza Sandwich, 50
Pork
  Air-Fried Pepperoni Pizza
    Bagels, 148
  Breakfast Flats, 33
  Hawaiian Pizza Rolls, 72
  Loaded Tater Tots, 20
  Peach Bourbon BBQ Bacon-
    Wrapped Scallops, 86
  Pepperoni Bread, 138
  Piggies in a Basket, 156

Pizza Sandwich, 50
Shrimp and Spinach Salad, 58
Potato Balls, 128

Potatoes
Curly Air-Fried Fries, 132
Garlic Air-Fried Fries, 124
Loaded Tater Tots, 20
Potato Balls, 128
Roasted Potatoes and Onions with Herbs, 136
Salmon Croquettes, 49

R
Ricotta Pancakes, 34
Roasted Chickpeas, 168
Roasted Green Beans, 114
Roasted Potatoes and Onions with Herbs, 136

S

Salad
Chicken Waldorf Salad, 54
Shrimp and Spinach Salad, 58
Strawberry Poppy Seed Chicken Salad, 64
Salmon and Crab Cakes, 106
Salmon Croquettes, 49

Sandwiches
Chicken Parmesan Sliders, 68
Chocolate Monkey Sandwiches, 141
Classic Patty Melts, 66
Foxy Face Foldovers, 152
Hawaiian Pizza Rolls, 72
Hearty Veggie Sandwich, 70
Mushroom Po-Boys, 60
Nashville-Style Hot Chicken Sandwich, 56
One-Bite Burgers, 74
Pizza Sandwich, 50
Tasty Turkey Turnovers, 144
Turkey Dinner Quesadillla, 62
Savory Stuffed Tomatoes, 110
Shortbread Cookie Sticks, 146
Shrimp and Spinach Salad, 58

Side Dishes
Air-Fried Cauliflower Florets, 122
Air-Fried Corn-on-the-Cob, 124
Bang-Bang Cauliflower, 118
Cheesy Garlic Bread, 134
Cinnamon-Honey Glazed Carrot Chips, 109
Crispy Brussels Sprouts, 122
Curly Air-Fried Fries, 132
Garlic Air-Fried Fries, 124
Garlic Air-Fried Mushrooms, 110
Garlic Knots, 126
Garlic Roasted Olives and Tomatoes, 134
Italian-Style Roasted Vegetables, 120
Olive Twists, 114
Pepperoni Bread, 138
Potato Balls, 128
Roasted Green Beans, 114
Roasted Potatoes and Onions with Herbs, 136
Savory Stuffed Tomatoes, 110
Simple Golden Corn Bread, 116
Stuffed Air-Fried Avocado, 112
Zucchini Tomato Rounds, 130
Simple Golden Corn Bread, 116

Snacks
Air-Fried Bowtie Bites, 166
Everything Seasoning Dip with Bagel Chips, 164
Guacamole with Corn Tortilla Chips, 162
Kale Chips, 172
Lavash Chips with Artichoke Pesto, 170
Roasted Chickpeas, 168
Toasted Tortellini, 161

Spinach
Hearty Veggie Sandwich, 70
Lemon-Pepper Shrimp on Garlic Spinach, 92
Shrimp and Spinach Salad, 58
Turkey Dinner Quesadillla, 62
Steak Fajitas, 102
Steak, Mushrooms & Onions, 88
Strawberry Banana French Toast, 36

Strawberry Poppy Seed Chicken Salad, 64
Stuffed Air-Fried Avocado, 112
Sweet Cocktail Meatballs, 12

T
Tasty Turkey Turnovers, 144
Toasted Pound Cake with Berries and Cream, 175
Toasted Ravioli, 28
Toasted Tortellini, 161

Tomatoes
Breakfast Pepperoni Flatbread, 42
Burger Bites, 18
Caprese Portobellos, 24
Garlic Roasted Olives and Tomatoes, 134
Island Fish Tacos, 98
Mini Pepper Nachos, 22
Savory Stuffed Tomatoes, 110
Zucchini Tomato Rounds, 130
Tuna Pies, 156

Turkey
Breakfast Pepperoni Flatbread, 42
Tasty Turkey Turnovers, 144
Turkey Breast with Roasted Squash, 90
Turkey Dinner Quesadillla, 62
Turkey Breast with Roasted Squash, 90
Turkey Dinner Quesadillla, 62

V
Veggie Pizza Pitas, 154

Z
Zesty Italian Chicken Nuggets, 100

Zucchini
Hearty Veggie Sandwich, 70
Italian-Style Roasted Vegetables, 120
Turkey Breast with Roasted Squash, 90
Zucchini Tomato Rounds, 130
Zucchini Tomato Rounds, 130

METRIC CONVERSION CHART

VOLUME MEASUREMENTS (dry)

$\frac{1}{8}$ teaspoon = 0.5 mL
$\frac{1}{4}$ teaspoon = 1 mL
$\frac{1}{2}$ teaspoon = 2 mL
$\frac{3}{4}$ teaspoon = 4 mL
1 teaspoon = 5 mL
1 tablespoon = 15 mL
2 tablespoons = 30 mL
$\frac{1}{4}$ cup = 60 mL
$\frac{1}{3}$ cup = 75 mL
$\frac{1}{2}$ cup = 125 mL
$\frac{2}{3}$ cup = 150 mL
$\frac{3}{4}$ cup = 175 mL
1 cup = 250 mL
2 cups = 1 pint = 500 mL
3 cups = 750 mL
4 cups = 1 quart = 1 L

VOLUME MEASUREMENTS (fluid)

1 fluid ounce (2 tablespoons) = 30 mL
4 fluid ounces ($\frac{1}{2}$ cup) = 125 mL
8 fluid ounces (1 cup) = 250 mL
12 fluid ounces (1$\frac{1}{2}$ cups) = 375 mL
16 fluid ounces (2 cups) = 500 mL

WEIGHTS (mass)

$\frac{1}{2}$ ounce = 15 g
1 ounce = 30 g
3 ounces = 90 g
4 ounces = 120 g
8 ounces = 225 g
10 ounces = 285 g
12 ounces = 360 g
16 ounces = 1 pound = 450 g

DIMENSIONS

$\frac{1}{16}$ inch = 2 mm
$\frac{1}{8}$ inch = 3 mm
$\frac{1}{4}$ inch = 6 mm
$\frac{1}{2}$ inch = 1.5 cm
$\frac{3}{4}$ inch = 2 cm
1 inch = 2.5 cm

OVEN TEMPERATURES

250°F = 120°C
275°F = 140°C
300°F = 150°C
325°F = 160°C
350°F = 180°C
375°F = 190°C
400°F = 200°C
425°F = 220°C
450°F = 230°C

BAKING PAN SIZES

Utensil	Size in Inches/Quarts	Metric Volume	Size in Centimeters
Baking or Cake Pan (square or rectangular)	8×8×2	2 L	20×20×5
	9×9×2	2.5 L	23×23×5
	12×8×2	3 L	30×20×5
	13×9×2	3.5 L	33×23×5
Loaf Pan	8×4×3	1.5 L	20×10×7
	9×5×3	2 L	23×13×7
Round Layer Cake Pan	8×1½	1.2 L	20×4
	9×1½	1.5 L	23×4
Pie Plate	8×1¼	750 mL	20×3
	9×1¼	1 L	23×3
Baking Dish or Casserole	1 quart	1 L	—
	1½ quart	1.5 L	—
	2 quart	2 L	—